Total Business Planning

Third Edition

Total Business Planning

Third Edition

A Step-by-Step Guide with Forms

E. JAMES BURTON, PhD, CPA, CFE
Executive Director, Jones Chairs of Excellence
Professor of Accounting
Middle Tennessee State University
Murfreesboro, TN

WILEY

John Wiley & Sons, Inc.
New York • Chichester • Weinheim • Brisbane • Singapore • Toronto

Library of Congress Cataloging-in-Publication Data:

Burton, E. James.
    Total business planning : a step-by-step guide with forms / E. James Burton. — 3rd ed.
        p.   cm.
    Includes index.
    ISBN 0-471-31629-6 (pbk./disk : alk. paper)
    1. Business planning.   I. Title.
HD30.28.B84   1999
658.4'012—dc21   99-11248

Printed in the United States of America.

10 9 8 7 6 5 4 3 2 1

Contents

Preface

Earlier versions of this book enjoyed great success due in large measure to those clients and users who took the time not only to use them, but also to suggest improvements. Like all good products, this book is in a state of continuous improvement. In this iteration there are four specific improvements I would like to point out:

1. The addition of the visioning process
2. The availability of Powerpoint slides via the Internet to be used by a planning facilitator choosing to use this book as the planning model
3. The addition of more information on the budgeting process
4. The inclusion of a disk with electronic versions of all of the forms in the book

I have continued to learn from clients and users of these materials. One of the things I have learned is that the visioning process is as difficult for senior managers as the implementation and follow-up is for those whose job it is to make the details of the plan work. So, this revision takes a careful, and hopefully helpful, look at creating a vision.

The addition of a computer disk brings this book well into the information age. It is amazing to realize just how far we have progressed in the few years since the first edition of the book, published in 1988. To my knowledge, there is no other planning resource that provides the types of tools required by the facilitator to accomplish the difficult task of getting the plan done. You too will find these tools of great help. I look forward to your feedback so that I can improve future editions of the book.

My adding a section on budgeting was not an obvious choice. Being that I am an accountant, budgeting seems like a fairly obvious process. But the more I work with managers from nonfinancial backgrounds, the more I realize the process is not intuitive. Therefore, a section on budgeting, placed in the proper planning context, seemed appropriate and has been added.

Finally, this revision was more difficult because Blan McBride was not part of the process. In the many years we worked together, Blan was my friend, colleague, partner, and, sometimes mentor. I miss having the opportunity to collaborate with Blan. Certainly, my life and the earlier versions of this book are richer because of him. I wish Blan and Eleanor McBride all the very best life can bring—they deserve it.

E. James Burton

Introduction

Using This Process

Obviously, there are many, varied types of organizations which want and need to create plans. The process described and forms provided in this book are effective for a wide range of organization types. On the following pages, we will describe different scenarios of planning needs and how to use this book if your case is similar to one of these.

The scenarios we will describe are:

The small, start-up business

The small, ongoing, single-product business

The larger, limited-product business which is functionally divided (sales, marketing, production, administrative, etc.)

The larger, multiple-product business which is functionally divided

The large, multiple-product business with largely autonomous divisions

The project or venture to be started within an existing business of any size

The not-for-profit entity

We will also refer to and describe nine **Levels** in the planning process:

1. Vision
2. Philosophy and Mission
3. Strategic Plan (Competitive Analysis)
4. Corporate Objectives
5. Planning Unit Goals
6. Tactics and Projections

7. Budgeting
8. Coordination
9. Implementation and Follow-up

Each **level** consists of multiple steps in the process; the term **level** is used to break the continuous planning process into discrete parts. Individual action plans, accountabilities, and performance evaluations may be linked to appropriate levels in the planning process.

The Planning Process: 9 Levels

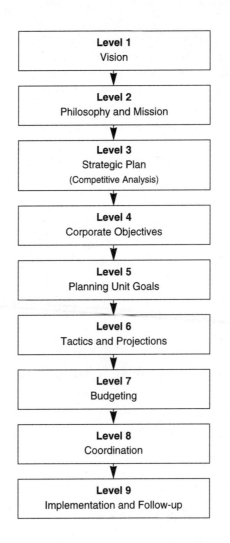

| **Level 1** |
| Vision |

| **Level 2** |
| Philosophy and Mission |

| **Level 3** |
| Strategic Plan |
| (Competitive Analysis) |

| **Level 4** |
| Corporate Objectives |

| **Level 5** |
| Planning Unit Goals |

| **Level 6** |
| Tactics and Projections |

| **Level 7** |
| Budgeting |

| **Level 8** |
| Coordination |

| **Level 9** |
| Implementation and Follow-up |

The Small, Start-up Business

Two pitfalls trap more start-up businesses than any others: lack of adequate capital and lack of experience in the business. Even a mediocre business plan will help highlight these problems, and the planner can either correct the deficiencies and proceed or postpone the venture until provisions are made.

In this case, the planning units are individuals, and each individual may have several functions to cover. The organization chart probably looks like:

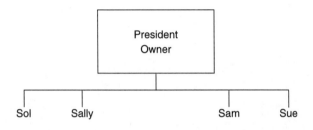

We recommend that a new venture focus its attention on:

Level 1 Vision

Level 2 Philosophy and Mission

Level 3 Strategic Plan (Competitive Analysis)

Level 4 Corporate Objectives

Additional, thorough attention should be paid to these prospective financial matters: cash flow projections, pro forma balance sheet, and pro forma income statements.

Without diminishing the importance of the remaining **levels**, the above describes the portions most helpful to the entrepreneur and most often initially requested by potential financing sources.

The Small, Ongoing, Single-Product Business

We assume that the key manager and/or owner of the business is active and participates in decisions throughout this type of business. The areas of the business are usually small and interact regularly and closely with each other. The organization chart may look like:

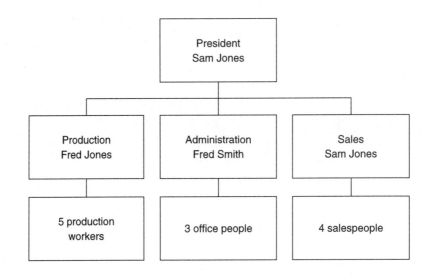

Because the business is small, it may not have distinct departments with managers over each. The planning units are quite possibly individuals. Therefore, **Levels 4** and **5** will merge into a single level where the corporate objectives are divided directly into action plans by people specifically assigned by top management. That is, the objectives are not separated into department goals, but rather the assigned person constructs an appropriate action plan from which individual accountabilities emerge. The department goals (**Level 5**) step is eliminated.

One plan covers the whole business because it is not large enough for different agenda to have developed. Also, there are not enough resources to spread out over more projects.

The Larger, Limited-Product, Functionally Divided Business

This is a classic scenario for using the total process described. The planning units are the functional areas, each of which has a key person at its head. While there may be more than one product, the company is probably geographically together and the organization chart may be similar to:

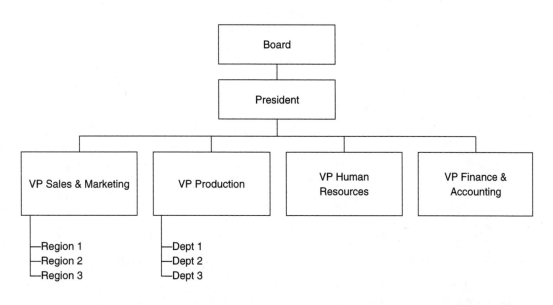

Because the vice-presidents are probably involved in **Levels 1** through **5**, our process should work very well. We recommend the full process in such cases. Corporate officers' accountabilities and performance evaluations are linked to every level in the process (**Levels 1** through **8**). Accountabilities and evaluations of departmental managers are linked to **Level 5** and **Level 6**, and those of individuals to **Level 6**. Communication of all pertinent parts of the plan is typically good and no large problems are likely.

The Larger, Multiple-Product, Functionally Divided Business

A typical organization chart might be:

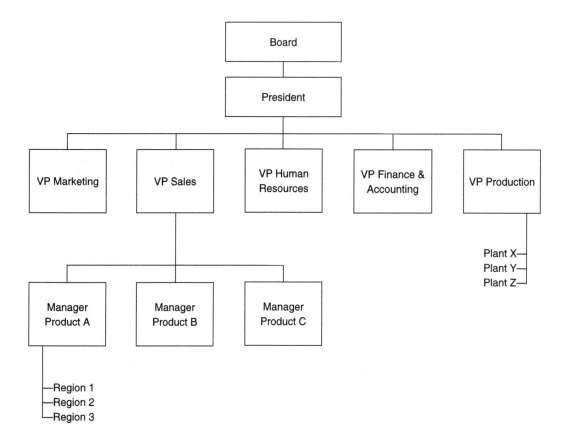

In this scenario our process works very well, provided there is open communication of **Level 1** through **Level 4** from top management to the product managers and plant managers, *and* between the product managers and plant managers. Also, it will probably be necessary for the product managers to be actively involved in **Level 3** relative to their specific product concerns.

Unfortunately, it is sometimes the case that organizations such as this require business plans from the product managers without having first created **Levels 1, 2, 3,** or **4.** Or they have created these without communicating them to these managers even if the information is requested by the managers.

When business plans are required from parts of the organization in this manner, only two real possibilities exist:

1. The person may attempt to write a plan without regard for the rest of the company. In this case, the manager typically starts the planning process at **Level 5** and creates short-term plans that are mostly budgets.

2. The person may decide that planning within such a context is not likely to be fruitful. Therefore, one will attempt to create what one believes **Levels 1, 2, 3,** and **4** are or would be if senior management did them. These are then placed into the plan with a notation that they are the foundation for the plan. If the assumed vision, philosophy, mission, and/or objectives are wrong, the remainder of the plan probably will not suit senior management either.

If, in this case, each product manager submits a business plan complete with vision, philosophy, mission, and corporate objectives that agrees with each other and with senior management's view, fantastic! If they submit plans with widely varying vision, philosophy, mission, and objectives, senior management should at least be aware of the problem that exists.

However, the product and plant managers have no real alternative but to follow (2) above. To the extent that cooperation and coordination among the plant and production managers is possible, the resultant submitted plans will be more consistent and more realistic, as well as more likely to be accepted by senior management.

The Large Multiple-Product Business with Largely Autonomous Divisions

A typical example of an organization chart for this circumstance is:

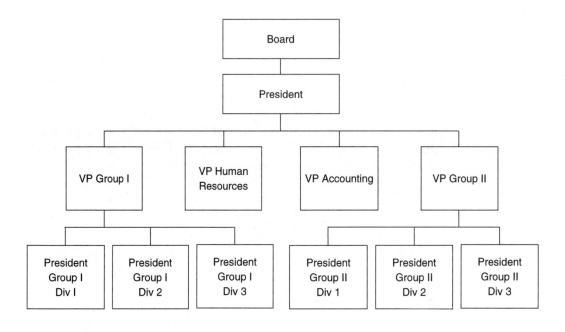

In instances such as this, the case may be:

1. The two groups are so diverse that any plan that covers both must be very general and is usually financial in nature. Therefore, at the corporate level the plan consists primarily of a broad vision, mission and philosophy, and financial objectives for each group. Then, each group takes this information into consideration when formulating its own plans. The group vice-presidents and the division presidents constitute senior management under our planning process and a plan using **Levels 1** through **9** is formulated for each group.
2. Not only are the groups diverse, but the divisions are also diverse. For the most part, the corporate level is a service organization and a banker. Each division is basically a company unto itself. In such cases, each division will create a complete and independent plan. Probably, the corporate plan will either roll up the divisional plans or will largely be an encompassing budget for all of the functions.

The Project or Venture within an Existing Business

Project planning is very similar to business planning in most respects. It is particularly close to business planning in the start-up business case. However, there are some differences:

1. This situation does not require the development of **Level 1** or **2**. The project should be working within the already established (written or not) company vision and philosophy. Often, the term *mission statement* will be used as the reported *reason for being* of the proposed idea. That is appropriate.

2. **Level 3** (Strategic Plan), on a limited and directed scope basis, is appropriate for new products or new businesses. For some types of project plans (new facilities, equipment changeovers, product line extensions, territory expansions, etc.), it may not be necessary at all.

3. Of course, the project or venture should be consistent with **Level 4** (Corporate Objectives), but no work at this level is necessary.

4. Primarily, this type of plan begins with **Level 5** (Planning Unit Goals). Such plans are usually operational in nature and quite detailed. **Level 6** (Tactics and Projections) and **Level 7** (Budgeting) normally will complete the planning needed for this scenario.

5. **Level 9** (Implementation and Follow-up) is particularly important. Often such projects are of a short-term, critical nature and the timing of dependent events is very tight. Therefore, **Level 9** becomes more important.

The Not-for-Profit Entity

While there are accounting differences between for-profit and not-for-profit entities, in many other respects they are quite alike. Perhaps the other single most striking difference is the use of volunteer rather than paid help that creates not only an operational but also a planning distinction.

In the not-for-profit situation, it is very important to involve as many people as possible in the planning process. In particular, it is important that the planning process include key volunteers and not just paid staff. Certainly, there are some not-for-profit entities that are large enough to function with mostly paid staff. In these cases, planning usually works as in the small, ongoing, single-product case with the additional involvement of the Board of Directors at **Levels 1** through **4**.

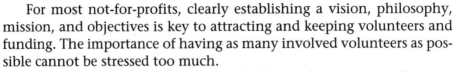

For most not-for-profits, clearly establishing a vision, philosophy, mission, and objectives is key to attracting and keeping volunteers and funding. The importance of having as many involved volunteers as possible cannot be stressed too much.

Another often overlooked area in not-for-profit planning is Strategic (competitive) Planning. The not-for-profit entity often has competition from for-profit as well as other not-for-profit entities in the service it provides for customers/clients. It also has competition for the funding it seeks. Therefore, competitive analysis is urgent.

Level 5 and **Level 6** work much the same in not-for-profit as in for-profit. The biggest difference has to do with getting things done through volunteers and the special problems that consequently arise.

Level 7, putting the numbers down, shows where funds are expected to originate and where they will go. This is critical for all organizations but perhaps especially so for not-for-profit ones.

Level 8, getting it on paper, is important for the not-for-profit. A thoughtful, well-documented plan can be useful for attracting funds and volunteers.

Level 9, making it happen, is probably the hardest part in such organizations. Because of the problems of getting volunteers to do what is needed, the implementation is often dependent upon a paid staff person's ability to motivate volunteers.

Summary

Overall, the circumstances of business plan development can be categorized into three groups:

1. Plans developed to tell those who do not have direct control over you, what you intend to do—possibly with help from them (bankers, venture capitalists, parent companies, foundations, etc.)
2. Plans developed for the purpose of helping you determine what you want to do and to justify the feasibility of it
3. Plans developed as an operating guideline and measurement tool for everyone connected with the organization

The process outlined herein, modified accordingly, can be effectively implemented in all of these circumstances.

Frequently Asked Questions (with Answers) About Business Planning

1. When the Vision, Philosophy, Mission, and (perhaps even) Objectives of Senior Management are either not developed or not communicated downward, what should middle managers do?

   Unfortunately, this is not uncommon. Although this is discussed in the section Using This Process, *it bears some additional consideration. Some things a middle manager can do are:*

   a. Request an example plan to use for format.

   b. Request a format outline that the person requesting the plan would like to have.

   c. Request a copy of the vision, philosophy, mission, and objectives into which the plan is supposed to fit (this gives notice of your knowledge of the need for these).

   d. Use the process outlined in this book and create the whole plan, labeling the portions which should be given you by senior management as assumptions key to the plan.

   e. Start at **Level 5** of the process described in this book and ignore the rest.

2. Is it possible to do successful planning in the situation described above?

   Yes, it is possible but it is not very probable. Because there is no coordination across the various planners (department heads, product managers, etc.), the planning becomes management by objection. *Everyone does what she/he wants to do until, and unless, someone objects.*

   Even successful plans drawn up in this scenario are usually short ranged and narrowly focused. They are typically plans for improving operational efficiency rather than plans for increasing the scope of the business.

3. If middle managers cannot get a vision, philosophy, mission, and/or objectives from senior management, can they start at **Level 4** and call it a business plan?

   In our opinion, the results here are not really a business plan. That is not to say that they are not valuable. They do not really cover the whole business, but the results may satisfy senior management.

4. Isn't it feasible that each department/division of a company could have its own business plan in addition to the company plan?

   Yes! In fact they may have such plans even when there is no company plan. Please see Using This Process *for more discussion.*

5. What happens when the planning begins at the bottom or middle of the organization?

   In our opinion, this usually means that senior management is failing to exercise the leadership it should. However, if there is time and if there is dialogue, this process can still work. It takes longer and costs more but it can work.

   *Usually, senior management is saying, "Tell us what you can do (or what you want to do) and we'll tell you what we will let you do." If senior management will take the submitted plans (the results of **Levels 5** and **6**) and will carefully analyze, consolidate, and condense them as input into their **Level 1** through **Level 4** responsibilities, and will then communicate back, the process can be very successful.*

   Unfortunately, too often senior management does not synthesize the plans: they simply bind them together. When that is the case you have operational plans for departments/divisions but not a plan for the business.

6. Are there other planning models and what do you do with them?

   Obviously, there are many other models in use. Perhaps the most common model is the budget first *model. In this model, planners are asked to prepare and submit a budget. The emphasis is mostly on revenue (for profit center types) or costs (for cost center or service types). Then, if anything else is called for, a plan for meeting the budget is requested.*

   Sometimes a quota *model is used. A manager is given a number (sales, costs, volume) and is then told to prepare a plan to achieve this.*

   When these, or other similar models, are used, we suggest you learn the game and play by the rules. Generally the plans are not worth much, but no one pays attention to them anyway.

7. My company is doing pretty well and we have never had a business plan. How do I convince senior management that we need one?

   Truthfully, you probably will not convince management. In such cases, the most likely thing to create awareness of need is disaster, and you don't want that. But, without a plan, disaster is what you'll eventually get.

   Meanwhile, you can start project planning and show how well it works. You can clip articles or give books that discuss successful companies and how they plan. You can recommend courses or conferences on planning to your managers.

   But don't get too excited. It often takes disaster to start the process.

8. Is the business planning process for a non–revenue-generating division or department (Human Resources) the same as for a revenue generator?

Essentially, yes, it should be. If there are corporate objectives that are well stated, these objectives will include goals and action items for most, if not all, divisions/departments. While the nature of the goals for revenue and non-revenue divisions/departments will differ, the process of constructing them need not.

In the situation in which a nonrevenue division/department is required to construct a separate business plan (without sufficient direction from or consultation with senior management) the situation changes somewhat. Management of such a division/department will need to delineate clearly its reason for being in the company and will need to create the most quantifiable, measurable objectives and goals possible.

It is often the case that business plans in this scenario are being used to justify decreasing or eliminating a division/department. Well-stated, measurable objectives and goals which show the cost–benefit relationships of the division/department may help stabilize or even improve the position of such a division/department. (See Using This Process.*)*

Particular attention should be paid to creating a strong mission statement that fully integrates the division/department into overall operations. Communication with revenue-generating divisions/departments to ensure their satisfaction with the product, and their mention of it in their plans, is also helpful.

9. We have never and still do not have time to plan. Things change too quickly and a plan would be obsolete before it could be implemented. Don't you agree that this negates any need for a plan?

    Frankly, rather than being a reason for not planning, this situation simply says that someone does not know how to plan or what a plan is intended to accomplish.

    A business plan that is created three to six months before the start of the year, which is exactly on target in all its estimates and in all its methods of action by year end is either:

    a. Being forced as a hard-and-fast rule rather than a guideline, or

    b. For a highly unusual situation

    Business plans are first and foremost a means of considering, in advance, as many probabilities as possible, selecting from among them the ones you want to make happen, and determining the means for doing so. These are always based upon assumptions. When and as the assumptions change, the plans based upon them also change. But if the planning process was well done, such alternatives have already been considered so they do not come as a surprise.

It is true that a plan may become obsolete. Planning (the process) will never become so. Planning may be useless if:

1. *Senior management refuses to participate and give leadership.*
2. *Senior management limits discussion and does not foster creative, innovative thinking.*
3. *Middle management and below are not trained and educated in how to plan and how to manage by plan.*

10. We seem to be great at planning, even getting our objectives and goals down on paper. We just do not ever seem to operate according to the plan. How will this process help?

    Level 8 *has been designed as a direct response to this concern. Organizations often drift off plan rather than abandon the plan. This is frequently due to their failure to have appropriate measurements and monitoring devices built into the planning stage.*

    Careful attention to developing meaningful, measurable, monitorable objectives and goals and then breaking these into individual accountabilities to which you frequently refer as motivational tools will be very helpful in staying "on task."

Following is a set of terms which we have adopted for use in this book. The terms are certainly not universally used. If your organization is accustomed to using a different set of terms, do not be dismayed. Simply substitute your terminology for that which is included here. However, it is critical that you use a consistent set of terms and that everyone in the organization understands the terms and uses them in the same way.

You may wish to distribute these terms to all who participate in the plan.

Business Planning Terms

Vision. The view of the future of the organization, which stresses what the visionary wants the organization to become. It is the integration and synthesis of information with dreams.

Philosophy. The set of basic beliefs which establishes the parameters for the business and its personnel. It is a statement of what we do and what we do not do.

- Why are we in business?
- How do we do business?
- What do we do and not do as a business?

Mission. The primary focus of the business which answers the question,

- What business are we in?

Status. An assessment of the present position which answers the question,

- Where are we?

Strategy. A method or course of action for dealing with competitors. It can be either proactive or reactive.

- Who else is in this business?
- How do we relate to them?

Objective. An aim or end of an action; results to be accomplished. For the *business as a whole* it answers the question,

- Where does the business want to go?

Goal. A point toward which a planning unit strives; a step toward accomplishing an objective. For the *planning unit* it answers the question,

- Where does the planning unit want to go?

Tactic. Methods of using resources to reach goals. It helps to answer the question,

- How do we get there?

Projection. A quantitative estimate of the results expected from using various tactics, particularly those we expect to employ.

- What will it look like when we do get there?

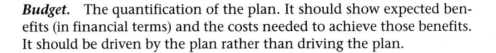
Budget. The quantification of the plan. It should show expected benefits (in financial terms) and the costs needed to achieve those benefits. It should be driven by the plan rather than driving the plan.

The Document

It is sometimes said that the major value to be gained from a business plan is not in the plan at all. Rather, 70 percent or more of the value comes from the *process* of planning. You will notice that the definition of business planning emphasizes the nature of the process. You will also note that a process is typically ongoing and continuous. While a business planning process should, in fact, eventually lead to a business plan, it does not stop at the point at which a plan is finished. The dynamics of the business environment ensure that a plan, once completed, will immediately start becoming obsolete. Therefore, it is essential to be prepared to revise the plan accordingly as new information is gathered.

While it is true that much of the value of planning lies in the process rather than in the product, it is extremely important that the process should eventually lead to a product. The business plan is a major medium by which the expectations of the organization are communicated both to the people within the organization as well as people without the organization. It ensures that the memories of those who were involved in the planning process stay consistent and it provides the opportunity for those planners to let others know what they intend to accomplish and how.

Sometimes a document is constructed and labeled a business plan. However, such documents are often, at best, budgets and not plans. You will note that a good business plan includes strategic or competitive planning, operational or efficiency planning, as well as financial planning. It should be made perfectly clear that the budget is the final phase of planning. The budget should come out of the plan rather than being an input to or a constraint on the plan. You will note this is the case in the process presented in this book.

Business Planning

Provides management with a realistic and systematic process:

1. To evaluate the present and desired status of the company
2. To evaluate the present and expected status of the competition
3. To identify assumptions on which to operate
4. To reconcile conflicting views

5. To arrive at agreed-upon
   a. Strategies
   b. Objectives
   c. Goals
   d. Tactics
   e. Projections

A Business Plan

1. Is the written product of the business planning process
2. Integrates strategic, operational, and financial (budgeting) planning

Comparison of Process Orientation and Product Orientation

Planning for Business	Business Plan
Having in mind; arranging the parts of; projecting the realization of	A proposed method of action or procedure
Specific to the planner	Written and available to all potential users
Often based on guesstimates rather than supported data	Carefully developed schedules to support projections
Not available as goal setting and motivating tool for others in organization	Goals and objectives for components and responsible individuals
Often focuses on areas of major interest to planner	Each area of organization integrated into plan
Not useful to outsiders	Effective for external financing and other needs
Process Only	**Process Leading to Product**

Recall the events of May 25, 1961. President John F. Kennedy gave a speech which began a process illustrating the *elements of a good plan*. His statement (paraphrased): "I believe this nation should commit itself to achieve the goal, before this decade is out, of landing a man on the moon and returning him safely to Earth." And we did! From the speech and from the space program that followed, we saw the elements fulfilled.

Elements of a Good Plan

Vision. *"A man on the moon . . ."* Our view of this today is quite different than it was pre-1961. Now it seems obvious. Children of the 1970s and 1980s take space travel for granted. But it was quite visionary at the time. Also note that it was probably not originally President Kennedy's vision. Most likely others much lower in government brought the vision to the President. His major contribution was not *creating* the vision but rather *communicating* the vision.

Commitment. *"And returning him safely . . ."* The President committed to those who would lay their lives on the line that every effort would be made to protect them. The astronauts needed to know that. They could then concentrate their attention on their tasks. The commitment was expensive. Extra tests were performed and numerous precautions were taken, but it helped get the job done.

Timelines. *"Before this decade is out . . ."* Overall, this was an unusual political statement. To box oneself into a specific completion time is generally not something a politician wants to do.

Phasing. *We had Mercury, Gemini, and Apollo.* When the effort to put a man on the moon began, the scientists and engineers did not immediately put people into capsules and begin launching them. Each step had a specific objective and the results of each phase were additive.

Contingencies. *Whatever can go wrong, will, and at the worst time.* With respect for those whose lives have been lost in the space program, throughout the lunar landing era the record was remarkably free of life-taking accidents. Considering the risks involved, the program performed beautifully. That was due largely to the painstaking contingency planning that tried (1) to imagine every possible problem, and (2) to create a plan first for preventing it and second for dealing with it if it happened.

Reporting. *"One small step for man, one giant leap for mankind."* As Neil A. Armstrong came down the ladder from the lunar module Eagle at 4:18 p.m. EDT on July 20, 1969, he made the above statement. This historic event, which included Edwin E. Aldrin, Jr. and Michael Collins as the other astronauts, is burned into the memories of all who observed it. And the camera that beamed those pictures back to Earth was not haphazardly placed. It was carefully staged to show this event, the objective of the program. Reporting should be keyed to the momentous events of the plan, not to the trivia.

Change. The plans that can and do change are the ones which last. One of the reasons for stating the assumptions on which a plan is based is that we can, from time to time, review those assumptions and determine whether or not a change of plan is needed. One of the best examples of a plan which includes a change process is the Constitution of the United States. While the United States is considered a young country it certainly has an old Constitution. Perhaps this Constitution has survived for 200 years because it contains the method by which it can be changed or amended. Similarly, business plans should contain within them the method by which they can be changed. This usually includes a quarterly review of assumptions and results, a determination of the changes which need to be made, and a listing of the changes which have been made.

It may be valuable to you as you go through the planning process to use the Elements page, such as the one following, to be certain that all of these elements are present.

After you have completed the process, but before you actually begin to write the plan document, fill out the Elements page in the appendix. Discuss it with the management team to be sure that your plan is what the team intends it to be.

You may choose to have each member of the **Level 1** team complete an Elements sheet (Exhibit A) independently and then compare and

---

EXHIBIT A   0001.doc

Elements*

Vision: _____

_____

Commitment: _____

_____

Timelines: _____

_____

Phasing: _____

_____

Contingencies: _____

_____

Reporting: _____

_____

Change: _____

---

*This form is also in the appendix.

consolidate them. This should ensure that all are operating on the same planning wavelength.

The following pages contain an outline for a general business plan. Obviously, plans constructed for special purposes may need emphasis or sections not shown here. Some industries may have elements of the business (research and development) that are important enough to warrant a section of the business plan.

The planning process should lead to a planning product. It is always better to have an understanding of the product being made before starting the process to make it.

You should give an outline of the plan (Exhibit B) to all the plan's contributors at the very beginning of the process. Then, they will all be working toward a common result.

EXHIBIT B

Business Plan Outline*

1. Cover Sheet
   a. Company name and/or logo
   b. Business plan and year
   c. Names (perhaps with phone numbers)

2. Sign-up Page

3. Executive Summary
   a. Two pages
   b. What's in it for the reader?
   c. How many different readers?

4. Table of Contents
   a. Make it detailed enough to be useful
   b. Should be about one heading per page of text

*This form is discussed further in the section on **Level 8** and appears in the appendix.

Exhibit B *Continued*

5. Major Assumptions
   a. Economy
   b. Suppliers
   c. Consumers
   d. Competition

6. History Section
   a. Two pages maximum
   b. Focus on relationship to plans
   c. Major events

7. Philosophy

8. Definition of the Business
   a. Usually less than one page
   b. What business(es) are we in?
   c. What is the glue holding us together?

9. Definition of the Market
   a. Consider buyers and sellers
   b. Can use strategic factors analysis to help describe sellers (competitive analysis)
   c. Describe buyers demographically, psychographically, and by distribution channel

10. Description of Products or Services
    a. Most emphasis on new ones
    b. Advertising information sometimes helpful
    c. No catalogs

11. Management Structure
    a. Show that you have the right people
    b. Quarter-page résumés
    c. Relate résumés to goals

(continued)

EXHIBIT B *Continued*

12. Strategies, Objectives, Goals, and Tactics
    a. Longest section of the plan
    b. Strategies lead to objectives
    c. Do not forget operational objectives
    d. Objectives lead to goals
    e. Format to reduce writing and ease reading

13. Financial Data
    a. This is the plan translated to dollars
    b. Budgets
       —Capital items
       —Cash flow
       —Revenue and expense
    c. Cost–volume–profit analysis

14. Appendices
    a. Supporting detail
    b. Making it work
    c. Not a dumping ground for superfluous pages

The Planning Communications Process

The planning process occurs in a series of meetings. We have divided these meetings into nine levels. Each level may require several meetings to accomplish the essential tasks. Each meeting should add value toward the final plan.

It is important that meetings be run efficiently and effectively. Someone should be in charge and attending to detail. For meetings of more than half a day the following Facilitator's Checklist will be helpful in ensuring proper tools for an efficient meeting.

Use the Facilitator's Checklist in Exhibit C and the Meeting Hints in Exhibit D. Give them to each person who will conduct one or more of the planning meetings.

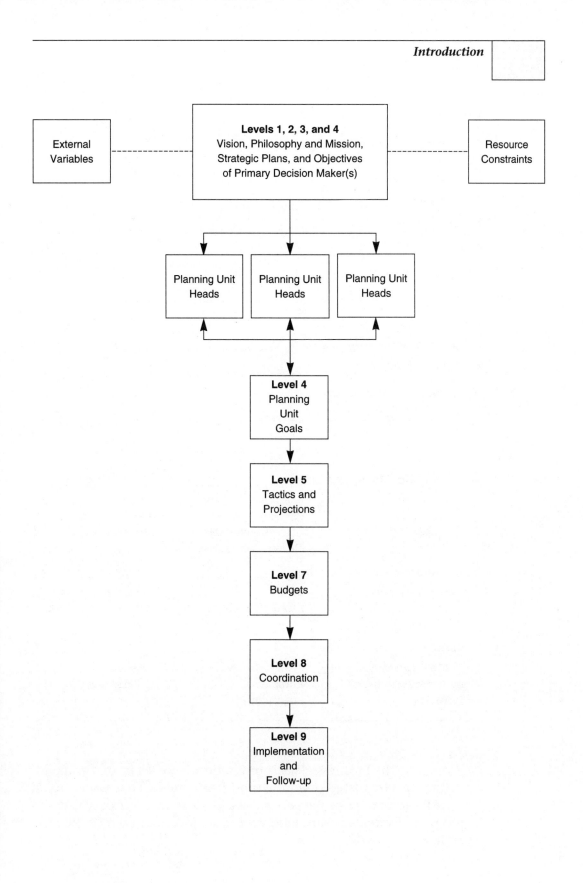

Exhibit C

0002.doc

Facilitator's Checklist

Meeting Checklist

Facility Name _____

Address _____

Phone _____

Facility Contact Person _____

Off-hours Contact Person _____

Limo: Phone _____ Cost _____

Car Rental On-site _____

Recreation Available _____ Cost _____

Directions to Facility (if necessary)

_____

_____

Meeting Room Name or Number _____

____ Ease of Access	____ Walls Okay for Tape	____ Rest Rooms Accessible
____ Noise Level	____ Windows Covered	____ Out-of-Room Phone
____ Visual Distractions	____ Chairs Comfortable	____ Break Service Specified
	____ Table(s) Substantial	

Dining Room Name or Number _____

____ Size Appropriate	____ Buffets	____ Adequate Servers
____ Separation from	____ Menu Checked	
Meeting Room		

Equipment

____ Flip Charts and	____ Note Pads	____ Markers
Stands (with backs)	____ Computers	(all necessary colors)
____ Pencils	____ Projection	

Complete the Business Plan Coordination Time Chart in the appendix using the completed one in Exhibit E as a guide. Give copies to all who are listed as responsible persons as a guide to the necessary times to be followed. Estimated completion times are given for each of the nine levels later.

Exhibit D

Meeting Hints: Dos and Don'ts

Do	*Don't*
1. Be sure the meeting is necessary.	1. Put more on the agenda than can be covered.
2. Be sure all the appropriate people are notified in writing.	2. Have the meeting at an inappropriate facility.
3. Be sure the agenda has been prepared and circulated.	3. Fail to check on the availability of needed services.
4. Be sure each participant knows what she/he is supposed to bring and to do.	4. Forget to have appropriate food service.
5. Start on time and end on time.	5. Create unnecessary problems of transportation or parking.
6. Keep minutes to summarize what happens.	6. Allow any one participant to dominate.
7. Identify the person in charge.	7. Allow any participant to be anonymous.
8. Use an off-site facility if possible.	8. Have spouses at the meeting.

Exhibit E

 0003.doc

Business Plan Coordination Time Chart*

Task	Responsible Person	Due Date*
1. Gather background data, including plans, budgets, financial statements, and performance evaluations for past five years (if available).	Plan facilitator	2 weeks
2. Level 1 See page 33	Visionary and Senior Management	Ongoing
3. Level 2 See page 39	Senior Management	4 weeks
4. Level 3 See page 51	Senior Management	4 weeks
5. Level 4 See page 59	Senior Management	2 weeks
6. Level 5 See page 75	Planning Unit Managers	4 weeks
7. Level 6 See page 91	Planning Unit Managers	4 weeks
8. Level 7 See page 99	Plan Facilitator and Budgeting Head	4 to 8 weeks
9. Level 8 See page 111	Plan Facilitator	4 weeks
10. Written presentation	As chosen	
11. Oral presentation	As chosen	
12. Level 9 See page 119	Plan Facilitator and Planning Unit Managers	Monthly or quarterly

*Indicates approximate time needed for the first plan attempt. Obviously, many factors can affect these estimates. Provide a total horizon of *not less than* four months (preferably six months).

**Depending upon to whom the presentation is made, this may be the plan coordinator, a planning unit manager, or even senior management.

The nine levels of meetings for building a business plan are illustrated in the following sections. Relevant forms, not completed, are duplicated in the appendix for your use.

These sheets constitute *a plan for the plan*. When properly and fully completed they will provide a road map for the development of the plan.

Study the illustrative pages for understanding. Then, consider how you would complete these pages for your own plan.

The example pages will be repeated later for emphasis and continuity of process. They are presented here, all together, to give you a quick feel for the process in total.

The blank forms in the appendix and/or the accompanying disk of these forms are for your own planning process.

Level 1

Vision

Who: This is often the product of a single visionary—the owner, chief executive officer (CEO), or head of the organization. It is possible to "vision" by committee, but it does not seem to work very often. Usually, the vision is that of one person, but it may be refined by a group as they consider it.

What: A picture of the future that can be clearly communicated to others in the organization so they, too, can know what future the organization is working towards.

When: Vision does not come on demand. It is a process—a never-ending process of reading, thinking, dreaming, studying, and observing. It is a process of questioning and then looking for answers to those questions. It should be going on constantly. As the vision becomes clear, then it should be articulated to others who can and will challenge and refine it.

Where: It may be a good idea for the senior management team to go away and consider ideas. But, because this is an ongoing process, it happens not so much in special circumstances but in the daily routine.

How Long: For some, the vision never comes. They are so busy taking care of today they have no time to think about tomorrow. There is no time limit on vision. Take it as it comes. Work on it daily. Think about it constantly.

Level 2

Philosophy and Mission

Who: This is the job of the senior management team. The CEO, chief operating officer (COO), chief financial officer (CFO) (all of whom may be the same person), and his/her direct reports (at least) should be involved.

What: A clear, concise statement of the philosophy and the mission of the business. This should be done in not more than four pages. The mission statement should be one concise paragraph, although there may be some explanation regarding that paragraph.

   This is the foundation not only of the plan but also of the current business. Do not skimp here. Do not underestimate the value of this. Give it time and careful attention.

When: Since this is the foundation it must be done first. We suggest that you begin work on this as much as six months before you expect to have a completed plan in place. Do this first even if you are time constrained and must complete the plan in a shorter period.

Where: We recommend that the senior management team do this work in an off-site environment. Get away from the offices. Go to a hotel, a resort, or someone's private retreat. Better still, go to a conference center whose staff is trained to meet your needs.

How Long: This varies considerably depending upon how much advance work has been done, whether a philosophy and mission have been written before, and whether professional facilitators are involved. However, you should expect *not less than two days* strictly devoted to this. Use the remainder of the four weeks discussed earlier to review, disseminate, and discuss the results.

Level 3

Strategic Plan

Who: The people from **Level 2** must be involved. You may also wish to bring in staff people (if you have them) with special interest in this area. And you may want to include the top level operations and product people if they were not part of **Level 2.**

What: As you will see more clearly later, the term *strategic planning* means the development of a plan for understanding and dealing with competitors. While this does have long-range implications, it is not synonymous with the commonly used term, long-range planning.

Specifically, we are looking for those factors of competition which will create advantages for us in the marketplace. In order for this to occur, two things must be so: (1) The factor must be one of importance to the customer or client, and (2) It must be one on which we can clearly (and positively) differentiate ourselves from our competition.

When: As soon as possible after the completion of **Level 2.**

Where: The initial data gathering can be done from the office environment. However, when the decision-making time comes we prefer to do this in an environment as described in **Level 2.** The off-site setting lends importance and urgency to the discussions.

How Long: Assuming proper groundwork has been done (which may take several weeks), and appropriate competitive information is available, this is a two to three day session. The decisions made here affect every aspect of the business and should be given due diligence in the deliberations.

Level 4

Corporate Objectives

Who: Although this sounds repetitive, the fact is that the same people from **Level 2** should also be responsible here.

What: The U.S. Marine Corps advertises for *a few good men*. We believe you need *a few good objectives*. How many? There are no hard-and-fast rules but the number four seems reasonable. Often, two objectives are expressed in financial statement terms (e.g., profitability, return on assets, return on sales, gross margin, cost reduction, net worth, return on stockholders' equity). One is employee oriented (training, benefits, work environment, etc.); the other is project oriented (new plan, new territory, new product, etc.).

However many objectives you choose to state, each should be:

- Specific
- Measurable
- Clear
- Concise
- Positive
- Reasonable

- Actionable
- Relevant
- Monitorable
- Consistent
- Motivating
- Divisible
- Inclusive
- Timebound
- Congruent

When: You may be able to add this onto the **Level 3** meeting. However, we suggest that you not do that on your first attempt at building a plan. You need time to ratify **Level 2** and **Level 3** before setting your objectives. Therefore, we suggest a delay of two to four weeks following **Level 3**.

Where: If time and/or money is a problem this can be done on-site. However, we recommend going off-site if possible.

How Long: Depending upon the clarity of the Strategic Plan, this may take only one day. Plan on arriving midday and departing late the following afternoon. Again, however, although the process may culminate in one day, it will percolate over several weeks.

Level 5

Planning Unit Goals

Who: Generally, those who directly report to those involved with **Level 2** will be the main focus of this level (i.e., product managers, territory managers, plant managers, division managers, etc.).

What: Each planning unit should state at least one goal in support of each corporate objective. The real burden, at **Level 4**, is to develop objectives that are truly corporate and into which every planning unit can reasonably fit. Each goal should be a component block of accomplishing the objective which it supports.

When: The first three levels should be complete and should have been disseminated to these people before they begin work on **Level 5**. We suggest a minimum period of two weeks for feedback from these people after the products of **Level 2** through **Level 4** have been given to them. Once senior management is comfortable that **Level 2** through **Level 4** are reasonably solid, work can begin on **Level 5**.

Where: Separate meetings will first be held by individual planning units to construct their own goals. These should take place on-site because of the numbers and job requirements of the people. Once the planning units have developed their goals, the planning unit managers should meet for one day in an off-site setting to present their goals to each other for discussion, revision (if necessary), and adoption.

Of course, it is important that the adopted and approved goals add up to the accomplishment of the objectives. If they do not, either the goals or the objectives must be modified to make them all align.

How Long: As indicated above, there may be several different meetings of varying lengths involved here. Total elapsed time will often be about four weeks.

Level 6

Tactics and Projections

Who: The planning unit managers and their direct reports (this may go down to the first line supervisors).

What: Each adopted and approved goal should have an action plan with appropriate measurements and monitoring points for it. Since this is the *daily operational portion* of the plan, it will be detailed.

When: Work can commence on this level as soon as senior management has approved the product of **Level 5.**

Where: Because of the information needed and because of the numbers and job requirements of the people involved, these meetings will probably be held on-site.

How Long: There likely will be many short meetings (one to three hours) involved in the development of this part of the plan. Total elapsed time again may be about four weeks.

Level 7

Budgets

Who: The planning facilitator and whoever is charged with producing the master budget. The cooperation of all planning unit managers and others with budgetary responsibility is also essential. Managers who are accountable for the results of the plan should be responsible for the construction of the budgets. Generally, this means planning unit managers, in cooperation with those who report to them, should have responsibility for the most detailed budgeting and the process should roll up through the chain of command to successively higher levels.

What: The financial statement of the plan in sufficient detail to provide direction, monitoring, and feedback to planning unit managers and above as to the accomplishment of the plan. The exact format of the budget will be dependent upon the specific organization and its requirements. The result should be a series of documents which detail financial responsibilities at each level of the management hierarchy. Managers with only responsibility for cost controls will have only expense budgets. Managers with revenue responsibilities will prepare pro-forma income statements. Managers with capital responsibilities will prepare capital budgets as well.

When: As soon as possible after the completion of **Level 6** but not before. The plan should drive the budget, not the reverse. If the budget process begins before the goals and action plans are in place and accepted, the budget will drive the plan.

Where: This process should be done on-site where all necessary information is available.

How Long: This is very hard to predict. It is dependent on the size and complexity of the organization as well as the complexity of the budget you wish to develop. Seldom is the process complete in less than a month and some organizations take up to six months. If the plan is well in place and good records have been developed and kept, budget development should probably be completed in not more than three months.

Level 8

Coordination

Who: When it comes to completing the plan it is usually best to have one person designated to put it into document form. Whoever is so designated should have sufficient clout to require and obtain cooperation to get parts of the plan in as needed.

What: A written document following the outline given earlier. If possible, the basic text portion of the plan should be about 20 pages. The appendices may be as voluminous as necessary to support the plan.

When: The plan should be complete and in the hands of all responsible people 15 to 30 days before it is to become the operative document.

Where: Normally, the plan is completed (put together) in the office environment.

How Long: Finalization should not really be a large problem if the preceding steps have been well followed. Allow at least two weeks, and preferably four, to put the document together.

Level 9

Implementation and Follow-up

Who: The Facilitator and Planning Unit Managers will have the primary responsibility for this. However, it takes the cooperation of all parties to the plan to make it work properly.

What: The product of this process comes in two broadly identified parts: INPUTS and OUTPUTS. The forms contained in this section will assist you with the development of both of these.

When: This process must be initiated before the start of the period for which the plan is operative and continued throughout the planning horizon on whatever basis of regularity you determine is needed (probably not more than monthly nor less than quarterly). These ongoing review procedures should be completed as soon as possible after the completion of the period being reviewed, preferably within not more than two weeks of the end of that period.

Where: These procedures are of the on-site nature.

How Long: The initial input process should not take more than two weeks at the longest. The ongoing review inputs should be completed in a matter of a few days.

Vision

Now we begin to put the planning process into action. The **Level 1** vision elements (who, what, when, where, and how long) from the introduction section are repeated. You, the planning facilitator, should complete the blank version of this form found in the appendix and on the forms disk. As the facilitator, you may also want to build a file of articles and/or books you find on the vision process. Share these with senior management on a regular basis as a means of helping them to continue their efforts to prepare a vision for the organization. At the risk of suggesting things which will obviously become dated, consider the following list of articles as examples of the types of things you might like to consider collecting and providing:

- Ted Gautschi, "Organizational Vision Forges the Missing Link," *Design News,* May 20, 1996, p. 138[1].
- James R. Lucas, "Anatomy of a Vision Statement," *Management Review,* February, 1998, p. 22[5].
- Ron A. Wolf and David T. Gering, "Making Strategy Work," *Journal of Business Strategy,* March–April, 1998, p. 11[4].
- John C. Camillus, Richard T. Sessions, and Ron Webb, "Visionary Action: Strategic Processes in Fast-Cycle Environments," *Strategy & Leadership,* January–February, 1998, p. 20[5].
- John Welton and Bruce Cook, "Institutional Vision: A Prerequisite for Fund Raising Success," *Fund Raising Management,* November, 1997, p. 28[3].

You may also want to create a file of other information that might be useful for the visioning process. Articles on technology, new products or processes, different marketing strategies, new markets trends, and so forth may be helpful in determining what the organization should be like in the future. No specific examples are offered here because the types of things in which you should be interested are determined by the type of organization you are. However, a quick review of Internet sources will reveal a plethora of articles in these areas for almost any type of organization. In fact, the real problem is not a lack of information but rather the problem of sorting out what may be relevant to you.

Level 1

Vision 0101.doc

Who: This is often the product of a single visionary—the owner, chief executive officer (CEO), or head of the organization. It is possible to "vision" by committee but it does not seem to work very often. Usually, the vision is that of one person, but it may be refined by a group as they consider it.

What: A picture of the future that can be clearly communicated to others in the organization so they, too, can know what future the organization is working towards.

When: Vision does not come on demand. It is a process—a never-ending process of reading, thinking, dreaming, studying, and observing. It is a process of questioning and then looking for answers to those questions. It should be going on constantly. As the vision becomes clear, then it should be articulated to others who can and will challenge and refine it.

Where: It may be a good idea for the senior management team to go away and consider ideas. But, because this is an ongoing process, it happens not so much in special circumstances but in the daily routine.

How Long: For some the vision never comes. They are so busy taking care of today they have no time to think about tomorrow. There is no time limit on vision. Take it as it comes. Work on it daily. Think about it constantly.

Exhibit 1.1 is an example of a partially completed **Planning Process Assumptions** form. Each participant at each level should get a copy of the blank form (provided in the appendix and on the forms disk). The form is used to document assumptions made throughout the process. These accumulated sheets are very useful in several ways—not only to ensure that all are making the same assumptions but also to help prepare contingency plans in the event assumptions are violated.

Exhibit 1.1

0102.doc

Planning Process Assumptions—Vision

Since the planning process deals with creating outcomes by future actions, it is essential and necessary to make assumptions about events and circumstances outside the planners' control. These assumptions are critical to the plan.

Please complete this sheet for each key assumption you make.

Assumption	Probability of Assumption Being Violated	Impact if Assumption Violated
1. Company will not be taken over and will continue with essentially present management.	1. Low	1. Operating philosophies and policies will change.
2. Raw materials will remain available at about current level.	2. Low	2. Alternate inputs are available that will not change product from customer view.

Return a copy of this sheet to the plan facilitator who will provide a copy to the next level planners.

It is important to understand the process and the concept of visioning. Much has been written, but the truth is that visioning is more art than science. Thinking about what visioning is and what it means may be helpful.

Vision means seeing. When used in the context of an organizational vision, it requires the ability to see what others cannot or will not see or conceptualize. It looks beyond the typical operational horizon, beyond all the typical operational limitations. It integrates diverse variables such as time, technology, personnel, and more in new and perhaps unique ways.

Vision is about becoming. It may bear little resemblance to what is. While it is often a top-down process springing from the mind of a single visionary, such is not always the case. In fact, when the vision wells up from within, it is much easier for it to permeate the organization and to become a force majeure.

The time horizon of the vision depends upon the organization and the environment within which that organization functions. Some situations dictate that five years is a very long time because change occurs so rapidly. Computer software may be an example of this environment. In other cases, perhaps utilities, the time horizons are much longer.

Vision looks out as far as is reasonable and synthesizes a picture of what can be. The visionary will begin to see this picture so clearly that she/he will be able to communicate it to others and to cause them to want to be a part of making that vision a reality.

It must be emphasized that vision is not a forecast of what the future holds unless someone communicates the vision and there are plans and actions to cause it to happen. It is not the natural result of allowing things to take their course. It is a chosen path and a selected destination. All roads considered by the organization should be judged by how well they lead to this destination.

Passion is critical. The vision needs a champion who desires the vision with single-minded intensity and will let nothing keep the vision from becoming reality. At least one person in the organization, preferably everyone in the organization, must be passionate about the vision. In order for the vision to be integrated into the organization, it must be translated from a mind picture into a word picture, articulated precisely so others can hear it and translate it back into the same mind picture held by the visionary.

Vision is work. It is a never-ending process of reading, thinking, dreaming, studying, and observing. The visionary must watch for trends, see nuances, and recognize obscure connections and relationships. The visionary must ask question after question. When something is seen through the distance of a spotting scope, it must be brought as quickly as possible under the scrutiny of a microscope.

Unfortunately, the development of a vision does not lend itself well to any set pattern. Like any creative process, it is subject to flights of fantasy and moments of inspiration that seem to come without warning, often from unknown sources. Although it is difficult to give you a process that is sure to work for you, it is possible to give some examples of vision statements from other organizations. These may be helpful in stimulating your thinking processes.

For example, in its early days, Microsoft focused its vision on putting a computer everywhere—on desks and in homes. In 1997, the vision expanded to cover the broader reach of the personal computer, especially internet capabilities. (www.microsoft.com/corpinfo/corpprof.htm).

The Dupps Company, Germantown, Ohio, historically a manufacturer of equipment for the rendering industry, expresses its vision as follows:

> While maintaining the traditional values of our privately held company, The Dupps Company will be a world-class competitor in the design and manufacture of evaporation and liquid/solid separation systems and equipment with a significant share in each market segment selected. (www.dupps.com/mission.html)

In an industry touted to grow some sevenfold in 20 years, FedEx must be forward looking or face death by being left behind. In the 1997 Annual Report, Chairman Fred Smith expressed the company's "V3" strategy—Vision, Value, Virtual. The explanation of "V3" tells much about the kind of company Chairman Smith sees FedEx becoming in this 20-year window of extraordinary opportunity. (www.fedex.com/us/ about/annualreports/fy1997/letter.html)

Northwest Airlines says that it wants "to build the world's most preferred airline with the best people; each committed to exceeding our customers' expectations every day." The president of Northwest, John Dasburg, has described this as a destination to which they are going— not so much one at which they have already arrived. (www.nwa.com/ corpinfo/profi/vision.shtml)

Columbia/HCA, the healthcare giant troubled by government accusations and in a period of downsizing its hospital network during 1998, has said it is "building comprehensive networks of healthcare services in local markets, integrating various services to deliver patient care with maximum efficiency." (www.columbia.net/overview/indes.html)

Sometimes, the vision statement can be simple, direct, and one line. For example, Promus Hotel Corporation of Memphis, Tennessee, says it wants to be the "premier hotel company in the world." It intends to achieve this status by focusing on "high quality, consistent accommodations delivered as an outstanding value, 100% guaranteed service, and dynamic growth. . . ." (www.promus.com/cgi-bin/quot...\\Default. htm&stock.htm&quote.file)

Texas Instruments is a company constantly reshaping itself to the future. President and CEO Tom Engibous has a vision based on technology. "We see a future where all personal electronics are connected and speaking the same language—a digital language." The things that will aid Texas Instruments to realize its vision are value, growth, and improved financial stability. (www.ti.com/corp/docs/library/montgomery97.htm)

As you review these few examples, some things may become apparent. Visions of the future are leveraged off of the competencies of the present. Visions of the future take into consideration the political and business environment in which the business does and will operate. Visions of the future recognize the impact of technology on how the business should be in the future. Visions of the future include the people who must make the vision a reality. Visions of the future often (but not always—see Columbia/HCA) are focused on growth and the costs and benefits associated with that growth.

The **Visioning Questions** form that follows (Exhibit 1.2) will help you document answers and to track changes to some of these types of things. Answering these questions will not automatically produce a vision. However, answering these questions may help you to begin the process that will lead to a vision. One of the best ways to use these questions is to have several different people answer the questions independently, then to discuss the answers as a group.

You may want even more detailed information of visioning. If so, there are a number of books dedicated solely to this area. One you may find helpful is *Visionary Leadership* by Burt Nanus (Jossey-Bass, 1992).

EXHIBIT 1.2 **Visioning Questions**

1. What are our current core competencies? _____

_____

2. What can we leverage to build our future?_____

_____

3. How will the political environment in which we operate change in the next 10 years, and what impact will this have on our organization? _____

_____

4. How will the business environment in which we operate change in the next 10 years, and what impact will this have on our organization? _____

_____

5. What technological changes will impact our organization? What will these changes do to us? _____

_____

6. How can we capitalize on them? _____

_____

7. Who are the people that will lead the organization over the next 10 years?

_____

8. What are their best skills? _____

_____

9. Where will they want to take the organization?_____

_____

10. How big should the organization be? _____

_____

11. What resources will be necessary to achieve this size? _____

_____

12. What knowledge and skills do we organizationally possess that produce a competitive advantage for us? _____

_____

Philosophy and Mission

We repeat the **Level 2** form from the introduction section. You, the planning facilitator, should complete the **Level 2** page from the appendix or forms disk and be certain that all affected parties have a completed copy of it.

You should also give all of these people a copy of the **Business Plan Outline**, the **Elements** page (blank), and the **Business Plan Coordination Time Chart** (completed by you). Explain to the **Level 2** participants that they should bring the Elements page to the first meeting, *completed as they see fit*.

Have several blank copies of the Elements page at the first meeting to use in drawing a consensus.

Philosophy and Mission 0201.doc

Who: This is the job of the senior management team. The chief executive officer (CEO), chief operating officer (COO), chief financial officer (CFO) (all of whom may be the same person), and his/her direct reports (at least) should be involved.

What: A clear, concise statement of the philosophy and the mission of the business. This should be done in not more than four pages. The mission statement should be one concise paragraph, although there may be some explanation regarding that paragraph.

This is the foundation not only of the plan but also of the current business. Do not skimp here. Do not underestimate the value of this. Give it time and careful attention.

When: Since this is the foundation it must be done first. We suggest that you begin work on this as much as *six months* before you expect to have a completed plan in place. Do this first even if you are time constrained and must complete the plan in a shorter period.

Where: We recommend that the senior management team do this work in an off-site environment. Get away from the offices. Go to a hotel, a resort, or someone's private retreat. Better still, go to a conference center whose staff is trained to meet your needs.

How Long: This varies considerably depending upon how much advance work has been done, whether a philosophy and mission have been written before, and whether professional facilitators are involved. However, you should expect *not less than two days* strictly devoted to this. Use the remainder of the four weeks discussed earlier to review, disseminate, and discuss the results.

Earlier, we defined philosophy to be *the set of basic beliefs which established the parameters for the business and its personnel. It is a statement of what we do and what we do not do.*

It is usually easier to approach a statement of coherent philosophy by breaking down the elements of that philosophy into simple components. We have given statements of Business Philosophies written by companies in various lines of business. We suggest that you review these but withhold them from distribution to participants in your planning process until after they have attempted statements on their own. Following that is a Philosophy form. You will note that there are blanks at the bottom indicating that this is not intended to be an exhaustive list.

It is important that the statements written by your organization are meaningful to you. If the participants view these examples too early they may choose to adopt them without giving due consideration to their content and meaning. A blank form for your use is in the appendix and on the forms disk.

The **Planning Process Assumptions** form is repeated in Exhibit 2.1 as a reminder that it should be used at every level of the process. Give each participant a blank form to start each level and accumulate the completed forms. The discussion of assumptions is an important part of planning.

Business Philosophies

General Examples

Integrity: We believe integrity is the cornerstone of all our business relationships; therefore, we will expect all of our employees to be honest and forthright with our customers, our vendors, and with all others whom they may contact in the name of the business.

EXHIBIT 2.1

 0202.doc

Planning Process Assumptions

Since the planning process deals with creating outcomes by future actions, it is essential and necessary to make assumptions about events and circumstances outside the planners' control. These assumptions are critical to the plan.

Please complete this sheet for each key assumption you make.

Assumption	Probability of Assumption Being Violated	Impact if Assumption Violated

Return a copy of this sheet to the plan facilitator who will provide a copy to the next level planners.

Management: We believe management is the art of leading people to accomplish stated objectives; therefore, leadership qualities and demonstrated ability to accomplish objectives will be primary criteria by which we select and evaluate managers.

Planning: We believe planning is the art of preparing for change; therefore, we will use planning as a management tool to keep us prepared for those changes that must come.

Customers: We believe that nothing happens until you make a sale, and sales are made only to customers; therefore, we will place the satisfaction of our customers above every other business consideration.

Employees: We believe well-trained, highly motivated employees are the most important means of serving our customers; therefore, we will select, train, and reward employees who place customer satisfaction first.

Profit: Our ability to properly service our customers depends on long-term profitability; therefore, we will manage our business to create a responsible return on assets.

Growth: We believe growth is a logical consequence for a well-managed company; therefore, we will evaluate management on the profitable, orderly, controlled growth the company sustains.

Community: We believe a profitable, growing business should, from its abundance, invest in the community that sustains it; therefore, we will individually and corporately invest in selected philanthropic activities of our community.

We suggest that you distribute copies of the blank Philosophy page in the appendix and the Suggestions page following it to all participants of your **Level 2** planning meeting. We also suggest that you choose one or two example statements that best fit your company, and distribute them to the participants in order that they might better understand the nature of the statements expected.

For your information, a copy of the Philosophy page and Suggestions for Use have been included in Exhibit 2.2.

An objective review of the company is a valuable, even essential first step. In order to help you accomplish that first step we have devised three forms which are contained in the appendix: **What Do We Do Best?**, **What Need Do We Meet?**, and **Whose Need Do We Meet?** We suggest that you use these three pages in your **Level 2** planning meeting to get people thinking objectively about the company. Exhibits 2.3, 2.4, and 2.5 are examples of these forms.

The airplane goes along with the question, **What do we do best?** If you were to ask the participants the question, "What do airlines do best?" you would expect answers such as, "Fly people," "Fly cargo," "Take people from place to place," or "Lose luggage."

While all of the above may be true, none of them is a complete enough story. What airlines actually do is to move people and cargo from airport to airport. The interesting question is, "How many people really want to go from airport to airport?" Furthermore, how many people really want to send cargo from airport to airport?

This last question was asked by Fred Smith, the man who started Federal Express. The answer that he came up with was, "No one." That cargo had to be handled by a multiplicity of people was in fact a problem.

Airline parcel services were quick, but expensive and inconvenient. In order to get delivery of small parcels great distances and in short periods of time, it was often necessary to carry the parcels to an airport, consign them to an airline, and find someone on the receiving end to go to the airport and pick them up. Same-day service was available but the inconvenience and cost were limiting factors.

Exhibit 2.2

0203.doc

Philosophy

Rank

_____ Profits	_____
_____ Customers	_____
_____ Employees	_____
_____ Management	_____
_____ Community	_____
_____ Integrity	_____
_____ Growth	_____
_____ Planning	_____
_____ _____	_____
	_____
_____ _____	_____
	_____

Suggestions for Use

Philosophy

1. The list of topics may not be complete. Add different topics if appropriate.
2. Rank the topics in order of their importance to the company. Compare your ranking with others and discuss the differences.
3. Working with others, attempt to assemble a master list of topics and rankings upon which you can agree.
4. Working with others, write a short statement about each topic. It might follow the form: "We believe that . . . ; therefore, . . ." It usually helps later in the planning process to have included the *therefore,* since it can provide something to act upon.
5. Test the statements produced by asking employees to read them and then describe what changes might be produced in their jobs by acting on them. If few changes are suggested, you have probably done an excellent job of communicating or else the statements are in need of reconsideration.
6. Order the statements by the ranks assigned in suggestion 2, print them, and distribute them to employees before requesting their participation in the planning process.

EXHIBIT 2.3

0204.doc

What Do We Do Best?

Airlines move people and things from airport to airport. FedEx moves packages from where they are to where you want them.

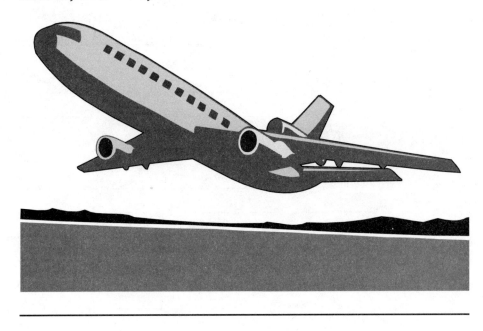

Recognizing a potential market, FedEx decided to pick up at the customers' site and deliver to the customers' destination. This amounted to a recognition that what the airline did best was not necessarily what the customer most wanted. When the customers' desires were recognized, the demand for the service increased dramatically.

Having decided *what we do best,* you must also decide if that meets the desires and needs of the consumer. Have the participants write down what they think your company does best. Discuss the answers and come to a consensus on the priority of the answers.

Exhibit 2.4 shows an old-style window shade. You have seen this type. They are made out of paper or vinyl on a recoil spring at the top. When you pull them down, you hope they will stay at approximately the level that you want. In his best-selling book *Megatrends,* John Naisbitt describes a company which in 1904 was manufacturing window shades. The company employed a consultant by the name of Mary Parker Follet to assist them. She asked the question, "What do you do?" and the response was, of course, "We make window shades." But her real question was, "Why do people buy window shades?"

EXHIBIT 2.4

0205.doc

What Need Do We Meet?

The end was light control. The means was window shades. It is important to understand customer needs from the ends, not only the means, point of view.

1904 Window Shades
Today _____

Light control Decoration

Heat control Privacy

You may want to ask participants, "Why do people buy window shades?" Expect answers such as, "To keep out the sun," "To keep out heat," "Privacy," "Security," or "Decoration."

Let's assume that this company determined that it was in the business of meeting the customers' need for light control, which was Ms. Follet's answer. Ask your participants to name products that are now available to meet this need and you will probably get a list that includes window shades, several varieties of blinds, awnings, tinting, electrical switches, light fixtures, and sunglasses.

Note the difference between the means (window shades) and the end (light control). Try to get the participants to determine what need(s) your company is in business to meet.

In a small Florida panhandle beach community, there is an amusement park. Such places are very fixed-cost oriented. Therefore, the owner wanted to get more customers into the park because each additional customer's entrance fee was mostly contribution margin going to meet fixed costs and to make a profit.

The park was surrounded by a wall and had a single entrance where the fixed price for all amusements was paid. The owner went into the park and observed the customers. Most were 8 to 15 years old. There was an even gender mix. From talking with many of them, he guessed the numbers to be about 60 percent local and 40 percent tourist, and he noticed they seemed to like the wilder, more exciting rides best.

With this information in mind, he decided on an advertising campaign. He chose a radio station that seemed to have the right audience. He gave a message telling listeners that they could meet their friends and have an exciting time there. He realized he needed exposure, so he ran the ads for several weeks. He found no change in his business.

One afternoon as he returned to his park, he happened to notice what was taking place out front. Mostly mature female drivers were delivering kids to the entranceway, waiting until they were in the park, and then driving away.

He quickly concluded that the kids in the park were not really the customers. Mothers were the customers—it was their needs he was meeting; his park was really a babysitting service.

EXHIBIT 2.5 0206.doc

Whose Need Do We Meet?

In the Florida panhandle amusement park example, the owner realized that *mothers,* not *kids,* had the *need.* Who purchases, or the most visible customer, may not be the real buying influence.

Using the Examples

Having gone through the three stories, the participants have considered three important questions individually. Now it is time to put these all together. Exhibit 2.6 is duplicated in the appendix. Use this form to come to a consensus on all of the four questions listed.

EXHIBIT 2.6

0207.doc

What Business Are We In?

1. What do we do best?

   We move people and things from airport to airport.

2. What need do we meet?

   People's desire to get things moved quickly.

3. Whose need do we meet?

   Business corresponders

4. What business are we in?

   We are in the business of rapidly moving business correspondence from airport to airport.

Suggestions for Use

What Business Are We In?

1. Answer question 1, considering both:
   a. What do we do better than anything else we do?
      and
   b. What do we do better than anyone else who does it?
2. Answer question 2, considering needs at a basic level and not a need for product or service.
3. Answer question 3, considering not just with whom you may come into contact, but also:
   a. Who really derives the benefits or has needs met?
      and
   b. Who actually pays and why are they willing to pay?
4. Answer question 4 by combining the answers to the first three questions. It may be possible to do this in one sentence. This answer may constitute your mission statement.
5. If your company is actually in several businesses, it is best to write a mission statement for each and add a statement describing the so-called glue which holds them together.
6. You may wish to add to the mission statement a description of the path the business may follow while growing. Growth could be along present lines, or it could require considerable change.

With this new revelation, he changed his advertising message and the station. He found the station many mothers listened to and he determined what was important to them (safety and price). His business improved dramatically.

Have your participants determine whose needs the company and its products/services really meet. Do not rest with superficial, easy answers. Probe into this as deeply as possible.

Mission Statements

General Examples

One of the major manufacturers in the United States has published the following:

> *Our mission is to improve continually our products and services to meet our customers' needs, allowing us to prosper as a business and to provide a reasonable return for our stockholders, the owners of our business.*

A wholesale distributor has stated:

> *We are in the business of providing on-time delivery of products which satisfy end user specifications and provide profitable margins to our distributors.*

A company with a bent for engineering among the senior managers determined:

> *We are in the business of profitably designing, manufacturing, marketing, and supporting products in which we have a value-added component.*

A small entrepreneurial operation wrote:

> *We are in the business of producing for elementary grade children supplementary learning materials which meet the following criteria:*
>
> - *integrate and coordinate with basic texts for skill development*
> - *are adaptable to student progress at the individual level*
> - *have been designed and tested by teachers*

A new business development group of a professional services firm thought:

> *We are in the business of creating new profit centers.*

An international, very large, specialty chemical company says:

Our mission is to balance value for our other constituencies with maximizing long-term shareholder value.

An international manufacturer of components and controls writes:

We produce products of high quality and value in the most competitively priced markets.

Strategic Plan

You, the planning facilitator, should complete the **Level 3 Strategic Plan** and be certain that all affected persons have a copy of it. Your blank form is in the appendix.

Also, you will want to distribute copies of the **Level 3 Planning Process Assumption** page from the appendix.

Strategic Plan   0301.doc

Who: The people from the **Level 2** meeting must be involved. You may also wish to bring in staff people (if you have them) with special interest in this area. And you may want to include the top level operations and product people if they were not part of **Level 2.**

What: As you will see more clearly later, the term *strategic planning* means the development of a plan for understanding and dealing with competitors. While this does have long-range implications, it is not synonymous with the commonly used term *long-range planning.*

Specifically, we are looking for those factors of competition which will create advantages for us in the marketplace. In order for this to occur, two things must be so: (1) The factor must be one of importance to the customer or client, and (2) it must be one on which we can clearly (and positively) differentiate ourselves from our competition.

When: As soon as possible after the completion of **Level 2.**

Where: The initial data gathering can be done from the office environment. However, when the decision-making time comes we prefer to do this in an environment as described in **Level 2.** The off-site setting lends importance and urgency to the discussions.

How Long: Assuming proper groundwork has been done (which may take several weeks), and appropriate competitive information is available, this is a two- to three-day session. The decisions made here affect every aspect of the business and should be given due diligence in the deliberations.

The process of formulating a strategic plan is difficult mostly because it requires a comprehensive look at all of the factors that impact the business. The strictly operational plan focuses itself internally and is, therefore, somewhat easier to make. In his excellent book *The Mind of the Strategist: The Art of Japanese Business* (McGraw-Hill, Inc., 1982), Kenichi Ohmae provides a framework for looking at the business environment. Certainly, Ohmae is not the only author in this area. A search of a major university library produced 265 postings with strategic planning in the title. Many of these are valuable resources. Even though the Ohmae book is somewhat dated, it is still an excellent work. We have adapted some of Mr. Ohmae's concepts to fit the formats that follow.

As is seen in Exhibit 3.1, the business strategy requires a careful look not only at the company but also at the customers and the competitors. We have divided each of the three large components into three subcomponents.

When considering the customers, it is necessary to think of the demographics (the customer's age, income, education, race, gender, etc.) and to get as accurate a picture on all pertinent factors as possible. It is also necessary to attempt to understand the psychographics (why the customer is a customer, why he/she buys, what his/her hot button is, what the buying motive is), and the channels to get to the customer (where the customer buys). This information is available from many sources—surveys, observations, warranty cards, and so on.

Without an understanding of the customer, any attempt at planning will be minimally successful. And any attempt at understanding competitors will be useless. By definition, a competitor is one who is vying for the same prize you are trying to win. And in business the prize is the customer.

With knowledge of who the customer is (or should be), the planning can look at the competitors. The subcomponents of the competition are listed as costs, volume, and function.

How much business (volume) is the competitor doing? Is this business that you could have or is it in targeted niches that are really not suited to your company? What advantages (or disadvantages) accrue because of this volume? What are the competitors' costs of doing business? Do they have manufacturing advantages or distribution advantages?

Describing the function of the competitors' products or services is another way of answering the question, "What need does this meet?"

E XHIBIT 3.1

The Three Cs of Business Strategy

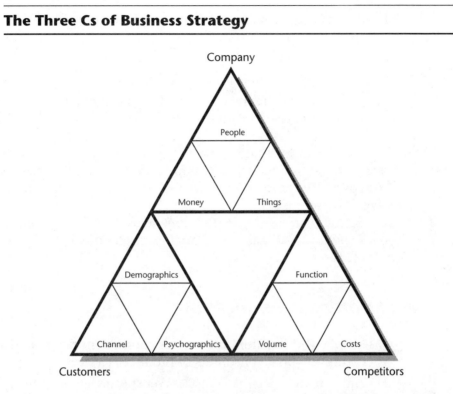

As a structural device, the equilateral triangle gains its strength from its balance. The legs are of equal length and the angles are also equal. Similarly, the balanced strategy gains its strength from not neglecting any of its three primary components: Company, Customers, Competitors. As shown above, we can use the same approach to strike a balance among the various parts of each of these components.

Here, the primary question is not "How does the product function?," but rather, "What does it do for the user?"

The strategic planning must also reflect on the limitations of the company. What are our people capable of accomplishing? Are we hindered by the people we have? What people do we need? Do we have the things (assets, capital equipment) necessary for the business we're in? What things must we have to accomplish our objectives? And where will the money come from?

Strategy

Is the formulation of a coordinated course of actions to gain superiority over competitors.

Strategic Planning

1. Should begin breaking the elements of the competitive environment into the simple components
2. Find those components which
   a. Are critical to the customer/client
   b. Are areas where the company has or can obtain superiority based upon the resources available

As the plan facilitator, you will probably need to lead the participants through the Strategic (Competitive) Planning exercise. Below are six steps for this process. We have included some forms to help you with some of these steps.

Use the blank forms in the appendix as you find them helpful to you. Exhibits 3.2–3.4 are some brief examples of what may go on some of these forms.

Steps in Strategic Planning

1. Describe the way the industry functions from raw materials suppliers through final consumers of products/services.
2. Complete the SWOT (Strengths, Weaknesses, Opportunities, Threats) Analysis (Company).
3. Complete the Strategic Factors Analysis (Competitors).
4. Complete the Thirty Questions Sheet (Customers).
5. Anticipate movement and changes by competitors and customers.
6. Create a plan of action.

Exhibit 3.2

 0303.doc

SWOT Analysis

Strengths	Weaknesses
1. Low fixed costs make us very price competitive.	1. Lack of depth of backup personnel.

Opportunities	Threats
1. Automation of certain functions will enhance response time and capacity as well as improve quality control.	1. Regulatory authorities are considering certain rules which will significantly increase our fixed costs while not affecting our competitors.

Exhibit 3.3

 0304.doc

Strategic Factors Analysis

Customer/Client

Product A
Product/Service

Rank	4	1	N/A	2	3	5
Companies	**Price**	**Quality**	**Delivery**	**Service**	**Technology**	**Distribution**
Our Company	1	2		4	4	1
Competitor A	2	3		1	2	4
Competitor B	3	1		3	1	2
Competitor C	4	4		2	3	3

(Suggestions for Use in appendix)

Exhibit 3.4

0305.doc

Thirty Questions to Assist with Strategic Planning*

1. Who are our five major customers (or classes of customers)?
   a. Road paving contractors
   b. City government
   c. County governments
   d. State DOT
   e. Private utilities

2. What are the common characteristics of these five?
   a. At times, need to close one lane of a two-lane road.
   b. _____
   c. _____

3. Why do they buy our product?
   a. Safety
   b. Pay back
   c. _____

4. Who are three potential customers (or classes of customers) who do not currently do business with us?
   a. Federal DOT
   b. Military
   c. Toll road operators

5. Why don't these three do business with us?
   a. Few two-lane roads
   b. Not labor sensitive
   c. Normally four-lane roads

*The complete thirty-question form appears in the appendix.

   When the strategic factors listed previously have been separately considered, it is time to interrelate them and formulate a course of action.

   A strategy is not an end unto itself. It is a means to an end—a way (and only one of many possible alternatives sometimes) to accomplish an ultimate objective. It is possible to accomplish the same objective with many different strategies.

   Strategic planning recognizes the various alternatives and begins to select from among them based upon the limiting factors previously discussed.

   After you have completed the materials in this section, you are ready to consolidate the process into a strategic planning product. You can accomplish this by completing the **Strategic Plan of Action** in Exhibit 3.5.

Exhibit 3.5 0306.doc

Strategic Plan of Action

With specific reference to your competitors, what do you most want to accomplish? (State the accomplishments as specific results.)

1. <u>Move to #1 in Quality</u>
2. <u>Move to #3 in Service</u>
3. _____

What course of action will you follow to cause these to happen?

1. a. <u>Automate the press line and eliminate human error.</u>
   b. _____
   c. _____

2. a. <u>Increase service hours available by 50%</u>
   b. <u>Decrease service response time to not more than 5 hours</u>
   c. _____

3. a. _____
   b. _____
   c. _____

Corporate Objectives

You, the planning facilitator, should complete the **Level 4 Corporate Objectives** page and be certain that all affected persons have a copy of it. A blank copy is in the appendix.

Also, give each participant a copy of the **Level 4 Planning Process Assumptions** page, found in the appendix.

Corporate Objectives 0401.doc

Who: Although this sounds repetitive, the fact is that the same people from **Level 2** should also be responsible here.

What: The U.S. Marine Corps advertises for *a few good men*. We believe you need *a few good objectives*. How many? There are no hard-and-fast rules but the number four seems reasonable. Often, two objectives are expressed in financial statement terms (e.g., profitability, return on assets, return on sales, gross margin, cost reduction, net worth, return on stockholders' equity). One is employee oriented (training, benefits, work environment, etc.); the other is project oriented (new plan, new territory, new product, etc.).

However many objectives you choose to state, each should be:

• Specific	• Clear	• Positive
• Measurable	• Concise	• Reasonable
• Actionable	• Consistent	• Inclusive
• Relevant	• Motivating	• Timebound
• Monitorable	• Divisible	• Congruent

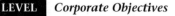

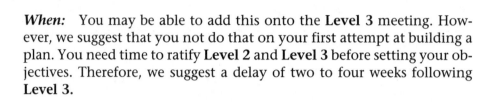

When: You may be able to add this onto the **Level 3** meeting. However, we suggest that you not do that on your first attempt at building a plan. You need time to ratify **Level 2** and **Level 3** before setting your objectives. Therefore, we suggest a delay of two to four weeks following **Level 3.**

Where: If time and/or money is a problem this can be done on-site. However, we recommend going off-site if possible.

How Long: Depending upon the clarity of the Strategic Plan, this may take only one day. Plan on arriving midday and departing late the following afternoon. Again, however, although the process may culminate in one day, it will percolate over several weeks.

The following pages in this section can be used to help with the formulation of the plan. You may choose to complete some of them yourself or to give them to others to complete.

History Questionnaire

Exhibit 4.1 is basic information for the plan—particularly for those recipients of the plan who are new to the company or are outsiders. You may want more historical information or you may find different historical data for different parts of the company—particularly those which have been acquired.

The basic question is "How did we get to be who we are today?"

Evaluation Chart for Planning

Exhibit 4.2, which has an instruction page with it in the appendix, is intended as a means to stimulate communications. From it you should be able to develop some objectives. Additional helpful forms included are:

- Where Are We?
- Where Are We Going?
- Status Quo Questionnaire
- How Do We Get There?
- How Do We Know When We Are There?

Review each of these sheets. Ask yourself who can provide the most information by considering and answering these questions. Probably, you

Exhibit 4.1

 0403.doc

History Questionnaire

To be completed by: _Sam Someone_

Completing these questions will help to show how we became what we are and why we are positioned to do what we have planned to do.

1. Date of company's founding. _____

   _____

2. Original founder(s) of business, name of business, location of business, and purpose of business. _____

   _____

3. Changes in name, location, and/or purpose, along with corresponding dates.

   _____

   _____

4. Major economic or environmental events which have affected company.
   1982 recession in mining—EPA crackdown on toxic emissions

5. Dates and explanations of major additions to or divestitures of business.

   _____

   _____

6. Major obstacles and problems the business has faced. _____
   Environmental cleanup in 1983

   _____

7. Turning points and causes of greatest periods of growth and profitability.
   1974 energy shortage

   _____

will want to give these to everyone involved at **Level 4** and ask them to complete the sheets before coming to the meeting. There is a blank form, with suggestions, in the appendix.

Exhibits 4.3 through 4.7 are primarily for your benefit as the plan facilitator. They will help you divide the relevant questions into workable pieces. You may want to reserve questions and ask them in the planning session.

EXHIBIT 4.2

 0404.xls

Evaluation Chart for Planning

Areas	Communications				Capital Investment													
	Clarity of Instruction				Production Equipment	Vehicles												
100																		
95																		
90																		
85					■													
80																		
75	■																	
70																		
65																		
60																		
55																		
50																		
45																		
40																		
35																		
30						■												
25																		
20																		
15																		
10																		
5																		

Instructions: For those elements of which you have knowledge, mark the appropriate square to give a score that answers the question "How are we doing with respect to this element?"

Exhibit 4.3

0405.doc

Where Are We?

To be completed by: _____

1. Why are we in business?

   _____

2. What business are we in?

   _____

3. Where are we in the life cycle of the industry?

   _____

4. Where are we in the life cycle of the company?

   _____

5. How did we get here?

   _____

   a. Narrative background of major events

   _____

   b. Historical financial information

   _____

6. What market factors affect us?

   _____

   a. Input side
      • Personnel

   _____

      • Materials

   _____

      • Financing

   _____

      • Equipment

   _____

(*continued*)

EXHIBIT 4.3 *Continued*

b. Output side
   • Primary customers

   _____

   • Secondary customers

   _____

7. What internal factors affect us?

   _____

   a. Our strengths

   _____

   b. Our weaknesses

   _____

8. What other external factors affect us?

   _____

   a. Regulation

   _____

   b. Legislation

   _____

   c. Competition

   _____

EXHIBIT 4.4   0406.doc

Where Are We Going?

To be completed by: _____

1. Who are the *we* referred to above?

   _____

2. What alternatives are available to us?

   _____

3. Consider the critical issues such as:
   a. Desired rate of growth

   _____

   b. Desired rate of profitability

   _____

   c. Desired public image

   _____

   d. New markets

   _____

   e. New products

   _____

   f. Availability of financing

   _____

   g. Capability of personnel

   _____

   h. Adequacy of plant and equipment

   _____

4. Where will our strengths take us?

   _____

5. What are our priorities?

   _____

EXHIBIT 4.5   0407.doc

Status Quo Questionnaire

To be completed by: _____

1. If the company operates in the coming year in the same manner as this year, identify those areas under your budgeting control (budget lines) which:
   a. Must be increased

   _____

   b. Could stay the same

   _____

   c. Are targets for cost reductions

   _____

2. Again assuming the present methods of operations:
   a. Identify two conditions over which you have little control that keep your area from making a greater profit contribution.

   _____

   _____

   b. State two changes which you have (or can get) authority to initiate that should make your area more profitable.

   _____

   _____

   c. By what date(s) could the above changes reasonably be made?

   _____

Exhibit 4.6

 0408.doc

How Do We Get There?

To be completed by: _____

1. What alternative courses are available to us?

   _____

2. What are the pros and cons of each alternative?

   _____

3. Which alternatives match up with our resources and our strengths (path of least resistance)?

   _____

4. What option(s) gives us the greatest future advantage?

   _____

5. Which objective is first priority?

   _____

6. Who will be responsible for each identified course of action?

   _____

7. What time frames should each have?

   _____

8. What is the biggest stumbling block to achieving our objective? Can we break it into more manageable problems?

   _____

9. What major external economic events (devaluations, political overthrows, nationalization, recessions, etc.) do we foresee?

   _____

10. What major internal economic events (acquisitions, divestitures, retirements, product demise, etc.) do we foresee?

    _____

11. What will it cost—dollars, people, dedication, etc.?

    _____

12. Do we have checkpoints and evacuation routes established?

    _____

(continued)

EXHIBIT 4.6 *Continued*

13. Is it consistent with our strategic plan?

_____

14. Can we monitor and measure our progress?

_____

15. Does this fit our stated philosophy?

_____

However, if you want to get written answers, copies of the pages are included in the appendix.

Exhibit 4.8 can be used in several ways:

- You can use it yourself as a means of directing provoking questions during the meetings to ensure that everyone is fully thinking through his/her suggestions.
- You can assign a particular person the responsibility of following up on each objective.
- You can disperse the lists to the participants as a guide.

EXHIBIT 4.7   0409.doc

How Do We Know When We Are There?

To be completed by: _____

1. Do you have a means to quantify your objectives and goals to the maximum extent possible?

_____

2. Do you have controls built into the planning process?

_____

3. Can you describe the final product in sufficient detail so that others can clearly picture what you are attempting to accomplish?

_____

4. Is the performance measure agreed upon?

_____

EXHIBIT **4.8**

Planning the Reports and Controls

Planning the Reports

1. Show the plan
2. Show the actual
3. Show the difference
4. Show period and year to date
5. Determine when to require explanations
6. Explanations include:
   a. Who is responsible?
   b. What caused it?
   c. Should it continue?
   d. What is to be done?
   e. When will it be done?
   f. Should the plan be changed? When?

Planning the Controls

1. What is to happen?
2. When should it happen?
3. When and how will we know if it is going to happen?
4. When and how will we know if it has happened?
5. Can we divide it into a series of events?
6. Are there points where we can reconsider?
7. Who is responsible for making it happen?
8. Who reports?
9. Are reports quantifiable?
10. Are reports verifiable?
11. What are the tolerances?

Each of these procedures has proven successful in different environments. Were we to choose only one, we would choose the third.

The **Internal Data Monitoring** sheet in Exhibit 4.9 is an example of information you may want to collect as a part of the planning process. The *Desired Pro Forma* column may present some objectives (or at least unit goals) that you will establish.

Collect the information in the first two columns and fill them in. Give the sheets to the participants and collectively determine what the numbers in the last column should be for the upcoming period.

If you desire, you can extend the pro forma for more periods.

The Internet has made access to data very different and very easy. Search engines allow an interested researcher to discover more "stuff"

Exhibit 4.9

0410.doc

Internal Data Monitoring

Item Monitored	Last Period	Current Period	Desired Pro Forma
Financial			
1. Profit Margin (Earnings/Sales)	.04	.037	.0425
2. Asset Turnover (Sales/Assets)	3.5	3.3	3.6
3. Capital Structure (Assets/Equity)	2.2	2.9	2.1
4. Return on Equity [(1) × (2) × (3)]			
5. Accounts Receivable Turnover (Sales/Accounts Receivable)			
6. Accounts Payable Turnover (Purchases/Accounts Payable)			
7. Current Ratio (Current Assets/Current Liabilities)			
Operational*			
8.			
9.			

*Examples of operational data to be monitored might include:

- Backlog
- Downtime
- Rejects
- Calls received

than anyone has time to digest. Be careful! Data available via the Internet is not always reliable. Check the source of the data. Be sure that whoever is making this information available is reliable. Also, remember that addresses change and information is sometimes removed from access.

Exhibit 4.10 represents a small sample of easily available sources that have been around for a long time, are generally thought to be reliable, and can be helpful in the planning process. Internet addresses have also been provided where available.

Of course, these lists are by no means exhaustive, but they may help you find some data of interest.

You may want to make these lists, with additions of particular importance to your industry and/or company, available to everyone involved in the planning process.

Exhibit 4.10

Sources of External Information

Federal Government
Many of the following and other general statistical sources can be found at
www.lib.utulsa.edu/guides/stage2.htm

1. Statistical Abstract of the United States
    (U.S. Department of Commerce, Bureau of the Census)
    Issued Annually
    Social, Political, and Economic Statistics
2. Survey of Current Business
    (U.S. Department of Commerce, Bureau of Economic Analysis)
    Issued Monthly
    Business Indicators, Domestic & Foreign Trade, Prices, Labor & Employment,
       Raw Materials
3. Economic Indicators
    (Superintendent of Documents, Government Printing Office)
    Issued Monthly
    Government Printing Office
    www.access.gpo.gov
4. Bureau of Census has several publications which are very helpful with demographics
    but most are issued on a ten-year cycle.
    www.census.gov
5. Federal Reserve Bulletin
    (Board of Governors of the Federal Reserve System)
    Issued Monthly
    Board of Governors' page has links to all federal reserve banks.
    www.bog.frb.fed.us

State Governments
State departments of commerce have data with a more local and regional orientation.
They can be especially helpful in gathering information on the availability and price of
labor.
    Generally, substitute the state postal abbreviation in the following example
address which is given for Tennessee (TN).
www.state.tn.us

Computer Accessible Data Bases
1. Data Courier, Inc., Louisville, Kentucky
    ABI/INFORM
2. The Center for Vocational Education, Ohio State University, Columbus, Ohio
    AIM/ARM

(continued)

EXHIBIT 4.10 *Continued*

3. Arthur D. Little Decision Resources, Cambridge, Massachusetts
   Arthur D. Little/Online
   www.arthurdlittle.com/cybrary/<u>cybrary home.html</u>
4. Business International Corporation, New York, New York
   BI/DATA Forecasts
   BI/DATA Timeseries
5. Bureau of Labor Statistics, United States Department of Labor, Washington, D.C.
   BLS Consumer Price Index
   BLS Employment, Hours, and Earnings
   BLS Labor Force
   BLS Producer Price Index
   //stats.bls.gov
6. Dun's Marketing Services, Parsippany, New Jersey
   D&B Dun's Market Identifiers 10+
   D&B Million Dollar Directory
   D&B Principal International Business
   www.dnb.com
7. Disclosure Incorporated, Bethesda, Maryland
   Disclosure II
   www.disclosure.com
8. Gale Research Company, Detroit, Michigan
   Encyclopedia of Associations
   www.gale.com
   Government data bases may be found at
   www.lsu.edu/guests/manship/classes/mc4971/data dir.html
9. Reports and Studies Index, Find/SVP, New York, New York
   Find/SVP
   www.findsvp.com
10. Bureau of National Affairs, Inc., Washington, D.C.
    Laborlaw
    www.bna.com
11. Predicasts, Inc., Cleveland, Ohio
    PTS Annual Reports Abstracts
    PTS F&S Indexes
    PTS International Forecasts
    PTS International Timeseries
    PTS Prompt
    PTS U.S. Forecasts
    PTS U.S. Timeseries
    Access available through subscribing libraries such as
    www.lib.duke.edu/databases/descriptions/fands.html
12. United States Department of Commerce, Washington, D.C.
    U.S. Exports
    Trade Opportunities
    www.stat-usa.gov

EXHIBIT 4.10 *Continued*

Lists of other resources may be found at:
www.umuc.edu/library/business.html
www.educaid.org/~chadwick/references/interbus.htm

Trade Associations
Besides periodicals and published studies, personal contact can be helpful here.
Prepublication information and even that which is not to be published is sometimes
available. Many have Internet presences.

Trade Publications
These publications are especially helpful for their (usually) annual statistical issues. May
have data available on-line.

Using Force-Field Analysis to Accomplish Objectives

Using force-field analysis to accomplish objectives is an idea for you, the
planning facilitator. During the meeting at **Level 4,** you may want to consider using the approach outlined on this page.

Force-field analysis, reduced to its simplest form, states that when
movement from one condition to another is desired, two sets of forces
operate: pressing and restraining. Many times, the easiest way to bring
about movement is to remove restraining forces rather than merely pressing harder.

To use this approach:

1. Identify objectives.
2. Identify restraining forces for each objective.
3. Group restraining forces by categories.
4. Find ways to remove or reduce restraining forces and categories, beginning with the weakest.
5. Set target dates for completion and name persons responsible.
6. Have follow-up meetings and/or reports soon after the target dates.
7. Do the above for the pressing forces.

With all of the information gathered so far, the biggest problem may
be to condense all of the possible, worthwhile objectives into just a few.
We suggest you get down to not more than five (we prefer four).

These five (or fewer) should be:

- Specific
- Measurable
- Actionable
- Relevant
- Monitorable

- Clear
- Concise
- Consistent
- Motivating
- Divisible

- Positive
- Reasonable
- Inclusive
- Timebound
- Congruent

Remember, objectives should be written in such a way that every planning unit can state one or more goals directly in support of the objective. Test each objective statement against the above list and rewrite it until it meets all the requirements.

Now you are ready to review the philosophy and mission, strategic plan, and objectives. If these are all consistent and stated as senior management wants them to be, distribute this information to all who will participate in **Level 5.**

Ask for feedback and be sure to give them a specific time. Modify any of these, if necessary, and give the **Level 5** people an approved set of this information before they start work at **Level 5.**

Planning Unit Goals

Level 5 is that portion of the process where the planning gets down to the nitty-gritty. Until now, senior management has been contemplating the accomplishment of the company as a whole. Some of the ends that have been espoused may appear exceptionally difficult and unlikely if not impossible.

At this point, the various responsibility units of the company (we call them planning units) divide the objectives into we-can-do-it pieces called goals. Goals are objectives divided into specific responsibility segments.

At the conclusion of the **Level 5** process, you should have a list of goals which, when put together, add up to the overall objectives.

If the objectives have been well written, all (or almost all) of the planning units will be able to state at least one goal in support of each objective. If this is not the case, the goals should be reconsidered. If the goals seem appropriate, the objectives may need to be rewritten.

As in the earlier levels, appropriate forms are included in the appendix and on the disk.

Planning Unit Goals 📀 0501.doc

Who: Generally, those who directly report to those involved with **Level 2** will be the main focus of this level (i.e., product managers, territory managers, plant managers, division managers, etc.).

What: Each planning unit should state at least one goal in support of each corporate objective. The real burden at **Level 4** is to develop objectives that are truly corporate and into which every planning unit can reasonably fit. Each goal should be a component block of accomplishing the objective that it supports.

When: The first three levels should be complete and should have been disseminated to these people before they begin work on **Level 5.** We suggest a minimum period of two weeks for feedback from these people after the products of **Level 2** through **Level 4** have been given to them. Once senior management is comfortable that **Level 2** through **Level 4** are reasonably solid, work can begin on **Level 5.**

Where: Separate meetings will first be held by individual planning units to construct their own goals. These should take place on-site because of the numbers and job requirements of the people. Once the planning units have developed their goals, the planning unit managers should meet for one day in an off-site setting to present their goals to each other for discussion, revision (if necessary), and adoption. Of course, it is important that the adopted and approved goals add up to the accomplishment of the objectives. If they do not, either the goals or the objectives must be modified to make them all align.

How Long: As indicated above, there may be several different meetings of varying lengths involved here. Total elapsed time will often be about four weeks.

Obviously, your starting spot for consideration of appropriate planning unit goals is the information developed in **Level 2** through **Level 4.** You should distribute this information to the planning unit managers as quickly as possible. Prepare a small package that includes the philosophy and mission, the strategic plan, and the objectives. You may also want to include information upon which these are based.

Request written feedback on these documents by a specified date. If any significant problems with these documents are noted, reconvene the appropriate people to review and revise as necessary.

When the **Level 2** through **Level 4** output has been confirmed, distribute the authorized version to the planning units and instruct them that this is the foundation for their planning effort.

Be certain that each planning unit manager gets at least one Planning Unit Goal Sheet for each objective set in **Level 4.** You will expect them to complete and return at least one such sheet for each objective. You may choose to type the objective on the sheets for them. If so, be sure to put only one objective per page.

Note there are three sample Planning Unit Goal Sheets near the end of this section.

Also included in this section are several sample analysis sheets. (In the appendix you will find clean copies followed by instructions for each.) Choose those which you think will be helpful to your people and give them to the planning unit managers as a part of the package you prepare as the authorized version of **Level 2** through **Level 4**.

If you are considering a planning retreat for your people, Exhibits 5.1 and 5.2 may be helpful. They are intended as general guidance only and should be modified to meet your needs. Exhibits 5.3 through 5.9 are very helpful in gathering and analyzing useful planning information. Exhibit 5.10 is excellent for summarizing intended goals on a single form.

EXHIBIT 5.1

Planning the Plan

A Planning Retreat Schedule
(A **Level 5** Example)

Day 1

Time*	Activity
One hour	Evaluation Chart for Planning completed: general historical review of company, major emphasis on past year's performance with comparisons to expectations
Two hours	Explanations of variances from expectations (confined to not more than 15 minutes per reporting division)
Two hours	Facilitator summarizes **Evaluation Chart for Planning** results and promotes discussion and consensus; summarizes the above to focus attention on common problems and opportunities.
One hour	Moderated discussion of anticipations of external events affecting business during planning horizon
Two hours	Subgroup meetings to establish unit goals for coming period

Day 2

Time*	Activity
Two hours	Each subgroup presents its unit goals for the next period (not more than 15 minutes each)
One hour	Facilitator leads discussion to find goal congruence and conflicts—each is listed
One hour	Facilitator leads discussion to align and prioritize goals as agreed
Three hours	Based upon consensus goals, subgroups meet to determine and coordinate tactics and resource needs
One hour	Facilitator summarizes above and seeks consensus; goals, tactics, and resource needs will be compiled into *Business Plan* for review

*Times are, of course, approximate. You may choose not to publish the time schedule to participants, but the facilitator should have time estimates from which to work.

Exhibit 5.2

 0503.doc

Input Factors Analysis

Item	Information	Indicator	Source
Personnel: • Management • Technical • Supervisory • Production • Support	Availability of people in our area qualified for entry level repair job.	Number of people graduating with AA or BA in Computer Science.	Placement offices of the following schools: a. b. c.
Financing: • Long-term debt • Long-term equity • Short-term			
Materials:			
Equipment:			

Exhibit 5.3

0504.doc

Input Factors Anticipation

	Administration
	Planning Unit
To be completed by:	P. Manager
Item	K4776 Interchange Control
Annual Quantity	180,000
Seasonal Variations	Jan–Jun. 10,000/month; Jul–Sept. 30,000/month; Oct–Dec. 10,000/month
Acceptable Substitute	K4776-B Interchange Knob

	Sources	
	Primary: Control Ind.	**Secondary:** Precision Knobs
Price Range	$1.47 each	$1.49 each
Lead Time	7 weeks	6 weeks
Availability	Constant	Sporadic

Anticipated Effects of Using Secondary Source or Substitute:

Costs additional 2¢ each for secondary—overprices competition

Quality not as good—20% higher failure rate

Sales/Marketing changes product appearance

Production no effect

Personnel no effect except quality assurance

EXHIBIT 5.4

0505.xls

Output Factors Anticipation

	Sales
	Planning Unit
To be completed by:	S. Manager

	Ours	Competitors				
		1	2	3	4	5
Price Range:						
Previous Year 1997	4.00–4.25					
Current Year 1998	4.10–4.25					
Next Year 1999	4.15–4.30					
Annual Quantity:						
Previous Year 1997	127,000					
Current Year 1998	129,000					
Next Year 1999	141,000					

Describe Anticipated Changes in:

Total Market Slow increase in total

Market Share Hold our own or lose slightly

Number of Competitors One or two new entrants with deep pockets behind them

Product Substitutes None seen

Advertising Levels Same

Customers Same

EXHIBIT 5.5   0506.xls

Product Planning Record

Manufacturing
_____
Planning Unit
_____
To be completed by: M. Manager
_____
Product X-Lon _____   For Year of 19<u>98</u>

		Year				
		1996	1997	1998	1999	2000
1) Units Sold	—Actual	297K	325K	450K		
2)	—Projected	400K	450K	475K	500K	550K
3) Unit Sales Price	—Actual	3.86	3.89	3.97		
4)	—Projected	3.75	3.82	3.94	4.05	4.09
5) Unit Variable Cost	—Actual					
6)	—Projected					
7) Unit Gross Margin	—Actual					
8)	—Projected					
9) Total Revenue	—Actual					
10)	—Projected					
11) Promotion Expense	—Actual					
12)	—Projected					
13)						
14)						
15)						
16)						

Problems may be indicated by:

- Declining number of units sold
- Declining total revenue
- Declining margins

- Increasing price reductions to maintain sales
- Increasing costs as a percentage of sales

- Increasing promotion expense as a percentage of sales
- Significant variances between actuals and projections

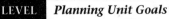
Exhibit 5.6

0507.xls

Salesperson's Sales Forecast for 1999

Sales

Planning Unit

To be completed by: ___Each Salesman___

Jones & Co.   H. Man

Customer   Salesman

Product(s)	Units Projected				
	Quarter 1	Quarter 2	Quarter 3	Quarter 4	Annual
X-Lon	400	425	550	400	1775
Y-Lon	375	390	375	450	1590
N-Lon	-0-	100	400	-0-	500
Totals	775	915	1325	850	3865

- Summarize by division
- Summarize by product

EXHIBIT 5.7   0508.xls

Sales Forecast Summary for 1999

	Sales
Planning Unit	
To be completed by:	_Each Salesman_

	Units Projected				
Product(s)	Quarter 1	Quarter 2	Quarter 3	Quarter 4	Annual
X-Lon	4,000	4,500	7,000	4,500	20,000
Y-Lon	3,900	4,000	4,100	3,900	15,900
N-Lon	4,100	4,000	4,500	4,000	16,600
Totals	12,000	12,500	15,600	12,400	52,500

Note the example sheets in Exhibit 5.11.

The goals stated on these sheets should support the specific objective to which they are related, and as previously noted for the objectives, they should be:

- Specific
- Measurable
- Actionable
- Relevant
- Monitorable

- Clear
- Concise
- Consistent
- Motivating
- Divisible

- Positive
- Reasonable
- Inclusive
- Timebound
- Congruent

Goals and objectives should be both doable and worth doing. It is the *so what?* test. If the objective or goal is accomplished and someone can still say "So what?," perhaps there isn't enough stretch in them.

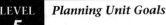

EXHIBIT 5.8

0509.xls

Value Analysis Grid

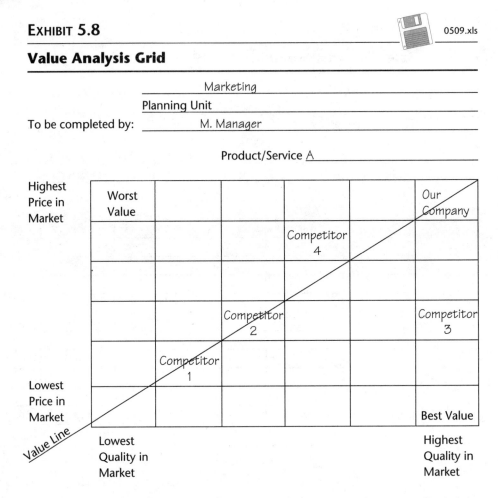

	Marketing
Planning Unit	
To be completed by:	M. Manager

Product/Service A

Competitor 3 may be a formidable opponent. They are equal to our quality but at a lower price. We will be very concerned with how they got there and whether a price war is about to break out. Do they have lower costs or are they sacrificing margins?

How did competitor 4 get where it is? Are they resting on reputation or did they get a perception of higher quality (and therefore price) through advertising?

Goals that do not have some resource requirements with them may indicate:

- The goal is trivial.
- The person does not understand what it will take to get the job done.
- The unit is fat and has resources that are not currently being used.

Any of the above suggest management should look closely at the area.

EXHIBIT 5.9

Value Analysis Grid

Marketing

Planning Unit

To be completed by: M. Manager

Product/Service B

This is obviously a *high end* product. Probably Competitor 1 is doing a knock-off and is capitalizing on the prestige of the product look-alike for those who cannot or will not afford the real thing.

Again, a determination of how we got where we are and whether we want to be there is quite important.

If each planning unit has completed one or more goal sheets for each objective you should have a substantial list of things to be accomplished.

Some planning units may have goals that do not specifically attach to any objective. These should be minimized and should be subject to more careful consideration than ones which do support objectives.

Remember, one of the aims is to focus the resources of the business on a few essential objectives in order to improve the probability of accomplishing them. Goals not in support of an objective tend to dissipate resources.

The sheet below is the end product of **Level 5** planning. Each planning unit should complete at least one such sheet for each objective stated in **Level 4.**

Exhibit 5.10   0510.doc

Planning Unit Goal Sheet

Objective _____   _____
_____

Goal _____   _____
_____

Present Status (/   /   )
_____

_____

_____

Resource Requirements
_____

_____

_____

Responsible Individual   _____

Estimated Completion Date _____

Concurring Managers   _____   _____

Authorized Approval _____

Comments   _____
_____

_____

_____

_____

Exhibit 5.11

Planning Unit Goal Sheet

Example 1

Objective Introduce X-Tron into three marketing territories by May 30, 1999

Goal Marketing Achieve a 15% awareness of X-Tron product and the standard "o" survey by Jan. 30, 2000

Present Status (6 / 30 / 98)

A before survey has been conducted and the awareness level now is approximately 3 percent.

Resource Requirements

$125,000 budget for media, literature, and trade shows.

Responsible Individual Marketing Support Manager

Estimated Completion Date January 30, 2000

Concurring Managers Sales Manager

Authorized Approval

Comments Because we already have products in these markets, we can coattail an existing market/sales contracts and literature.

Example 2

Objective Net income before tax of $2.3 MM for fiscal 1999

Goal Product 3 $20 million gross sales at 30 percent gross margin

Present Status (6 / 1 / 98)

Last year's sales were $18 million and margins were 27 percent. This was a period of penetration in two markets. Those markets are maturing and should yield slightly greater margins because our product is now proven.

Resource Requirements

Our primary need is for better literature. We must maintain our media campaign, even stepping it up slightly and we need four-color literature to leave with prospects.

Upgrade one sales position to sales manager.

Responsible Individual Sales Manager—Product 3

Estimated Completion Date End of year

Concurring Managers Marketing Manager

Authorized Approval

Comments This product fits our historic trends with product/market mix. There is no reason to expect it to deviate much from our norm. Our goal represents an 11 percent increase in sales and 11 percent improvement in margins.

(continued)

EXHIBIT 5.11 *Continued*

Example 3

Objective <u>Enhance each employee's job satisfaction skills</u>

Goal <u>Manufacturing Each department's employee will successfully pass all skills tests</u>
<u>on the Auto/Spot machine.</u>

Present Status (<u>6 / 30 / 98</u>)

<u>The department recently acquired the Auto/Spot welding machine. No employee has</u>
<u>yet been trained to use it.</u>

Resource Requirements

<u>One person will be dedicated full time as the trainee until all department employees</u>
<u>have been trained.</u>

Responsible Individual <u>Foreman</u>

Estimated Completion Date <u>June 15, 1999</u>

Concurring Managers <u>None</u>

Authorized Approval _____

Comments <u>This equipment will become the standard over the next three years.</u>

Collect the Goal Sheets from all planning units. Arrange them by objective (all goals that support objective 1, etc.).

On the Outline of Planned Changes sheet in Exhibit 5.12 list the goals by objective. Complete all columns.

1. Do the goals listed for each objective accumulate to assure the accomplishment of that objective? If not, either *stretch* some of the goals or *downsize* the objective.

2. Consider whether the results of the goals are worth the costs. If not, modify the goal or the means of accomplishing it accordingly.

3. Consider the timelines. Are they reasonable? Will they do what you need by when you need it?

Feed back any changes to the planning unit managers. Planning unit managers will use these approved goals as the basis for **Level 6.**

EXHIBIT 5.12

Outline of Planned Changes

0511.xls

#	Goals	Expected Results	$	Resources Required	$	Timelines			
						1st Qtr.	2nd Qtr.	3rd Qtr.	4th Qtr.
1	Increase Productivity	5% decrease in Direct Labor	1 MM	1 Press	500 K				

Tactics and Projections

Y ou, the plan facilitator, should have returned the Goal Sheets, revised as necessary, to the planning unit managers. Any substantive revision to the sheets should, of course, have been discussed with the manager as well.

You may also want to give copies of all Goal Sheets to all planning unit managers in order to keep them informed of the overall plan.

Once the planning unit managers have their approved goals back, it is time for them to complete the detailed action plans that go along with the goals. Obviously, the managers had at least a general plan of attack when they developed the goal. Now it is time to finalize that process.

You will want to give them blank copies of the Goal Action Plan Sheet (found in the appendix), as well as the completed examples included in this section. You will expect each manager to return a Goal Action Plan Sheet for each of their goals.

Tactics and Projections 0601.doc

Who: The planning unit managers and their direct reports (this may go down to the first line supervisors).

What: Each adopted and approved goal should have an action plan with appropriate measurements and monitoring points for it. Since this is the *daily operational portion* of the plan, it will be detailed.

When: Work can commence on this level as soon as senior management has approved the product of **Level 5**.

Where: Because of the information needed and because of the numbers and job requirements of the people involved, these meetings will probably be held on-site.

How Long: There will likely be many short (1–3 hours) meetings involved in the development of this part of the plan. Total elapsed time again may be about four weeks.

Examples of the **Goal Action Plan** forms for the planning unit are shown in Exhibit 6.1. These forms should indicate how, when, and at what cost the planning unit goals will be accomplished.

Each *Tactic* or *Action Step* assigned to an individual should also show up on that person's Individual Accountability and Action Plan sheets, shown in Exhibits 6.2 and 6.3.

EXHIBIT 6.1

 0603.xls

Goal Action Plan Sheet

Example 1

#	Tactics/ Action Steps	Responsible Person	Status/ Comments	Projections/ Evidence of Completion	J	F	M	A	M	J	J	A	S	O	N	D
									1998							
1	Tabulate results of *before* survey	JJ		Tabulation Complete	X											
2	Formulate market plan from (1)	JJ/AS		Plan submitted to PJ and approved		X	X									
3	Complete new media spot	BC	$40 K	Spot placed 3 times					X							
4	Complete new literature	BC	$35 K	Literature in hands of sales people							X					
5	Attend 3 regional trade shows	JJ	$42 K	Show attended/list submitted					X				X		X	
6	Conduct "Q" survey	JJ/Agency	$8 K	Survey complete w/15% awareness												X

Goal <u>Marketing Support Dept.</u>

	J	F	M	A	M	J	J	A	S	O	N	D
Report Date												
Date												
Initials												

EXHIBIT 6.1 *Continued*

Example 2

#	Tactics/ Action Steps	Responsible Person	Status/ Comments	Projections/ Evidence of Completion	1998												
					J	F	M	A	M	J	J	A	S	O	N	D
1	Trainee			Certificate of	X											
	Trained	MM		Completion												
2	Training Manual	MM/Trainer		Book Approved			X	X								
	Completed	Personnel		Personnel												
3	On-the-Job	Trainer/		Checklist Approved					X							
	Checklist	Personnel		Personnel												
4	Class 1–15 People	Trainer		Completed Classroom						X						
5	O-J-T Class 1	Trainer		Certificate							X	X				
6	Class 2–15 People	Trainer		Completed Classroom								X	X			
7	O-J-T Class 2	Trainer		Certificate									X	X		
8	Class 3–10 People	Trainer		Completed Classroom										X	X	
9	O-J-T Class 3	Trainer		Certificate											X	X
10	Dept. Celebration	MM/Trainer		Party												X

Goal <u>Manufacturing—Welding Dept.</u>

	J	F	M	A	M	J	J	A	S	O	N	D
Report Date												
Date												
Initials												

EXHIBIT **6.1** *Continued*

Example 3

#	Tactics/ Action Steps	Responsible Person	Status/ Comments	Projections/ Evidence of Completion	J	F	M	A	M	J	J	A	S	O	N	D
																1998
1	Complete New Product Literature	PT/LJ		Available to Field		X										
2	Identify New Sales Mgr. Prospect	PT		List of 3 to Personnel			X									
3	Select Sales Mgr.	PT		Position Filled				X								
4	Sales Mgr. Trained	PT/MK		Accepted Evaluation						X	X					
5	Implement New Price List	Sales Mgr.		Mailed to Customer								X				
6	Year-End-Sales Event	Sales Mgr.		Promotion Complete										X		
7	Sales Bonus Bowl	Sales Mgr.		Awards Mode										X	X	
8	Non-Discount Customers Target Program	Sales Mgr.		50 New Non- Discount Customers												X

Goal _Product 3—Sales Dept._

Report Date	J	F	M	A	M	J	J	A	S	O	N	D
Date												
Initials												

EXHIBIT 6.2 0604.xls

Individual Accountability and Action Plans

Name <u>John Doe</u>

Position <u>Salesman</u>

Evaluator <u>H. Man</u>   Date _____

Approved by _____ Date _____

Individual Accountability:
1. Improve territory unit sales by 10%

Individual Action Items:
1. Prepare customer prospect list.
2. Make at least 3 cold calls per week.
3.

Measurements:
1. List to H. Man by 1/15
2. Sales log

Performance Evaluation of Accountability:
(   ) More than   (   ) Satisfactory   (   ) Less than
     Satisfactory   Satisfactory

EXHIBIT 6.3   0605.xls

Individual Performance Evaluation

Name _John Doe_

Position _Salesman_

Dates of Review Period __/__/__ to __/__/__

Summary of Performance Evaluation:
(   ) More than   (X) Satisfactory   (   ) Less than
        Satisfactory   Satisfactory

Too New to Evaluate:
(   ) Satisfactory Progress   (   ) Unsatisfactory Progress

Action Plan Summary: (Use additional sheets if necessary)

Strong Points _Good planning and detail_

Weak Points _Follow-up on service problems_

Plan for Development _Enroll in Service School._

Evaluator's Signature _____ Date
Approved by _____ Date

Accountabilities Established:
   (   ) Accountabilities have been established for the upcoming period.
Evaluator's Signature _____ Date
Approved by _____ Date

Budgeting

The "what and how" of the plan should now be well in place. The objectives, goals, and action plans tell what is to be accomplished and how to accomplish it. Still missing is the quantification of "how much" both in terms of benefits and costs. This is a critical ingredient of the process, and now is the time to put it in place.

There is no one right process for budgeting. Virtually every organization that produces a budget has its own variations to the process. What will be shown in this chapter is a generic process which is representative of what is often done. Each organization specializes the budget process to fit its own needs. If you do not have a budget process already in place, this will give you guidance as to how to develop one. If you do have a process in place, this will provide a refresher to assure that all bases are being covered.

There are a number of budgeting resources available that will be much more detailed than this chapter. Naturally, any listing provided will become dated and need to be brought current. The following is provided as an example of available products only. You may want to refer to one or more of these for more in depth coverage of some areas.

- Robert Rachlin, *Total Business Budgeting: A Step-by-Step Guide with Forms,* John Wiley & Sons, 1991.
- Arthur V. Corr and Nancy Thorley Hill, "Preparation and Use of Budgets," Section D1, *Corporate Controller's Manual,* Paul J. Wendell, ed., Warren Gorham & Lamont, 1998.
- Eric James Burton and W. Blan McBride, *The Total Business Manual: A Step-by-Step Guide to Planning, Operating, and Evaluating Your Business,* John Wiley & Sons, 1991.
- Robert G. Finney, *Essentials of Business Budgeting: A Worksmart Guide,* American Management Associations, 1995.

- Terry Dickey, *Basics of Budgeting: A Practical Guide to Better Business Planning,* Crisp Publications, 1992.
- Jae K. Shim and Joel G. Siegel, *Budgeting Basics & Beyond,* Prentice-Hall, 1995.
- Robert Rachlin, et al., *Handbook of Budgeting,* John Wiley & Sons, 1993.

Software sources are changing constantly. Two sources found on the Internet are:

- Business Maestro, Planet Corporation, 1-800-366-5111
  www.planetcorp.com
- SRC Software, www.srcsoftware.com

Budgeting 0701.doc

Who: The planning facilitator and whomever is charged with producing the master budget. The cooperation of all planning unit managers and others with budgetary responsibility is also essential. Managers who are accountable for the results of the plan should be responsible for the construction of the budgets. Generally, this means planning unit managers, in cooperation with those who report to them, should have responsibility for the most detailed budgeting and the process rolls up through the chain of command to successively higher levels.

What: The financial statement of the plan in sufficient detail to provide direction, monitoring, and feedback to planning unit managers and above as to the accomplishment of the plan. The exact format of the budget will be dependent upon the specific organization and its requirements. The result should be a series of documents which detail financial responsibilities at each level of the management hierarchy. Managers with only responsibility for cost controls will have only expense budgets. Managers with revenue responsibilities will prepare pro-forma income statements. Managers with capital responsibilities will prepare capital budgets as well.

When: As soon as possible after the completion of Level 6 but not before. The plan should drive the budget, not the reverse. If the budget process begins before the goals and action plans are in place and accepted, the budget will drive the plan.

Where: This process should be done on-site where all necessary information is available.

How Long: This is very hard to predict. It is dependent on the size and complexity of the organization as well as the complexity of the budget you wish to develop. Seldom is the process complete in less than a month and some organizations take up to six months. If the plan is well in place and good records have been developed and kept, budget development should probably be completed in not more than three months.

The master budget process normally consists of two interrelated pieces—Operational Budgeting and Financial Budgeting. As the plan facilitator, you may be called upon to be involved in virtually all or none of these processes. Often, the controller, chief accountant, treasurer, or other financial person steps in to be the leader of the budget process. Certainly, the financial people should be involved and should provide significant help for budget development.

The level of budgeting required from different parts of the organization depends upon the responsibility assigned to the manager. A manager of a cost center—where the responsibility does not directly include the production of revenue—will be required to produce only a budget of the expenses expected for the upcoming period. A manager of a revenue center—where responsibility includes not only expense control but also revenue production—will be required to develop a budget which is essentially an expected income statement for that area of responsibility. These budgets, coming in from managers at the lower end of the management spectrum, once approved, will be aggregated to produce budgets of successively higher levels of responsibility. That is, the budgets are "rolled up" and additional information is added to them to produce the budget for the next higher level in the organization.

In general, the process might look something like Exhibit 7.1:

EXHIBIT 7.1

General Budgeting Process

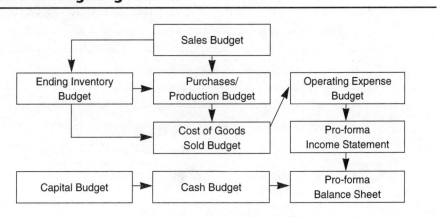

Although the graphic shows Sales Budget as the first step, it may be generalized to Revenue Budget. Where are the sources of revenue? How much is anticipated from each of these sources? This information should have been being developed as the action plans were being done. If new projects, products, or other revenue sources were included in the plan, these should be added to what is already known about the existing business. Those responsible for sales should produce these estimates after taking into consideration all of the plans for marketing, introduction of new products, changes in the marketplace, and so on.

Data from the **Product Planning Record**, the **Salesperson's Sales Forecast**, and the **Sales Forecast Summary** from **Level 5** should be particularly helpful in developing the sales/revenue projections. Those forms are presented in Exhibits 7.2 through 7.4 and on the disk.

With the information in hand as to what you expect to sell (whether products or services), you now can determine what you will need to purchase/produce. That purchase/production is dependent upon what you expect to sell plus what you want to have in inventory at the end

EXHIBIT 7.2

Sales Forecast Summary for 1999

	Sales
	Planning Unit
To be completed by:	Each Salesman

	Units Projected				
Product(s)	Quarter 1	Quarter 2	Quarter 3	Quarter 4	Annual
X-Lon	4,000	4,500	7,000	4,500	20,000
Y-Lon	3,900	4,000	4,100	3,900	15,900
N-Lon	4,100	4,000	4,500	4,000	16,600
Totals	12,000	12,500	15,600	12,400	52,500

Exhibit 7.3

Product Planning Record

	Manufacturing
	Planning Unit
To be completed by:	M. Manager
Product X-Lon	For Year of 1998

		Year				
		1996	1997	1998 Present	1999	2000
1) Units Sold	—Actual	297K	325K	450K		
2)	—Projected	400K	450K	475K	500K	550K
3) Unit Sales Price	—Actual	3.86	3.89	3.97		
4)	—Projected	3.75	3.82	3.94	4.05	4.09
5) Unit Variable Cost	—Actual					
6)	—Projected					
7) Unit Gross Margin	—Actual					
8)	—Projected					
9) Total Revenue	—Actual					
10)	—Projected					
11) Promotion Expense	—Actual					
12)	—Projected					
13)						
14)						
15)						
16)						

Problems may be indicated by:

- Declining number of units sold
- Declining total revenue
- Declining margins

- Increasing price reductions to maintain sales
- Increasing costs as a percentage of sales

- Increasing promotion expense as a percentage of sales
- Significant variances between actuals and projections

EXHIBIT 7.4

Salesperson's Sales Forecast for 1999

	Sales				
	Planning Unit				
To be completed by:	Each Salesman				
	Jones & Co.				H. Man
	Customer				Salesman

	Units Projected				
Product(s)	Quarter 1	Quarter 2	Quarter 3	Quarter 4	Annual
X-Lon	400	425	550	400	1775
Y-Lon	375	390	375	450	1590
N-Lon	-0-	100	400	-0-	500
Totals	775	915	1325	850	3865

- Summarize by division
- Summarize by product

less what you already have in inventory at the beginning of the process. That is,

Units to be sold + units desired in ending inventory – units in beginning inventory = Units to be purchased/produced in the current period.

The ending inventory budget is more a matter of plan than of calculation. That is, it is a matter of determining what you want it to be rather than letting the number be calculated. Of course, if you are determined to purchase/produce a certain amount during the period, then the following is true:

Units in beginning inventory + units to be purchased/produced – units to be sold = Units in ending inventory

The Cost of Goods Sold budget follows a similar pattern:

Cost of beginning inventory + cost of goods purchased produced = Goods available for sale

Goods available for sale – cost of ending inventory = Cost of Goods Sold

The Operating Expense Budget for each budgetary unit is a vital part of the overall budget. This budget should be *very* dependent upon the action plans developed in **Level 6**. Generally, operating expense budgets are prepared with considerable attention given to the actual results for the same budgetary unit from the previous period. These actual results are then modified based upon the best information about what will be different in the upcoming period. The previous history of the unit, the nature of the cost behaviors (that is, are the costs basically fixed and not subject to much change with changes in activity volume or are they variable and largely linked to the amount of activity), the activities to be performed and the expected volume of those activities will really drive the operating expense budget. Operating expense budgets should be as detailed as possible with all of the assumptions documented for future reference.

When the operating expense budget is complete the major sections of the income statement have also been completed and the proforma (expected or budgeted) income statement can be produced. The income statement looks like the following:

Income Statement

	Revenue
Less:	**Cost of Goods Sold**
	Gross Profit
Less:	**Operating Expenses**
	Income from Operations

Another important aspect of budgeting is the area of Capital Budgeting. Different organizations define "capital" items differently. Generally, whether an item is considered a capital item is dependent upon two factors—the length of the benefits to be received from the item and the cost of the item. If the item will be fully consumed and the benefits from it fully realized in a year or less, it is considered an expense item regardless of the amount it costs. However, if the benefits will last longer than a year, then the cost comes into play. Items that will have benefits lasting more than a year but have a cost below a given amount (determined by the organization) are still considered expense items. If the item's benefits will last longer than a year and the cost is above the threshold, then the item is a capital item. Usually, an item is a capital item if it must be depreciated. The process of determining what capital items will be acquired is referred to as *capital budgeting*. The definition of capital budgeting is roughly the same as the definition of economics—the study of the allocation of scarce resources to competing ends, over time, to maximize utility. That is, how do we best use our limited investment potential to make the most money.

With the income statement projected and the capital budget anticipated, the expected cash budget can be prepared. The cash budget recognizes not only where cash will come from and where it will be used but also the timing of those flows. In some organizations, cash flow is so critical that daily cash budgets are necessary. In other organizations, quarterly cash budgets may be more than sufficient. This depends on the organization.

The final piece of the budgeting puzzle is the proforma (expected or budgeted) balance sheet. This cannot be accomplished until all of the other pieces are completed because it requires numbers from all of them. The ending cash balance comes from the cash budget. Information relative to the fixed assets comes from the capital budget and the profit from the income statement is necessary to adjust the equity section of the balance sheet. Other pieces—accounts receivable, accounts payable, and so forth—come from other completed schedules.

The overall budgeting process often follows the following order:

- *Guidelines*. Top management communicates the parameters and expectations for the coming period.
- *First submission*. Planning units submit their broadly defined unit targets based on the goals and action plans developed.
- *Combination and review*. The first "roll-up" is performed to see how close to desired the first submission really is.
- *Negotiation and revision*. Based on their review, top management has conversations with unit management about changes needed to the budgets.
- *Second submission*. Unit managers revise their budgets to recognize the concerns of top management. (At this point the goals and action plans should also be revised to match the changes in the budgets.)
- *Additional iterations as necessary*. More negotiation, revision, and resubmissions may be needed.
- *Approval of top management*. At some point top management will "buy-in" on the submitted plans and budgets. These should become the basis for evaluation for the coming period. This is why it is es-

sential that the goals and action plans be altered to be consistent with the approved budget. (For example, if the original goal established required a new piece of equipment that was cut from the budget, then the goal and resulting action plans should be altered to accommodate this fact.)

Exhibit 7.5 is a general example of a budget. Because a budget is a financial model of the organization and every organization is different, the model for your organization will not exactly match this one. This one is provided for illustration only. Consult a more detailed source, seek help from a knowledgeable person, and/or get a good piece of software to assist you to develop the budgets specific to your organization.

EXHIBIT 7.5

General Example of a Budget

Sales Budget—Schedule A

	January	February	March	Total
Credit sales—80%	$56,000	$68,000	$72,000	$196,000
Cash sales—20%	14,000	17,000	18,000	49,000
Total Sales	$70,000	$85,000	$90,000	$245,000

Purchases Budget—Schedule B
Cost of goods sold is 60% of sales

	January	February	March	Total
Desire ending inventory	$15,300	$16,200	$ 9,000	$ 40,500
Plus cost of goods sold	42,000	51,000	54,000	147,000
Total needed	$57,300	$67,200	$63,000	$187,500
Less beginning inventory	–12,600	–15,300	–16,200	–44,100
Total Purchases	$44,700	$51,900	$46,800	$143,400

Cash Operating Expenses—Schedule C

	January	February	March	Total
Salaries and wages	$ 7,500	$ 7,500	$ 7,500	$22,500
Freight	4,200	5,100	5,400	14,700
Advertising	6,000	6,000	6,000	18,000
Other	2,800	3,400	3,600	9,800
Total Cash Operating Expenses	$20,500	$22,000	$22,500	$65,000

(continued)

EXHIBIT 7.5 *Continued*

Noncash Operating Expenses—Schedule D

	January	February	March	Total
Depreciation	$2,000	$2,000	$2,000	$6,000

Cash Collections—Schedule E
Usually based on historical information.

	January	February	March	Total
Cash sales—See **Schedule A**	$14,000	$17,000	$18,000	$ 49,000
Collections from prior months' sales	48,000	56,000	68,000	172,000
Total Cash Collections	$62,000	$73,000	$86,000	$221,000

Cash Disbursements for Purchases—Schedule F
Usually based on the way in which bills are anticipated to be paid.
50% in month of purchase and 50% following month—See **Schedule B**

	January	February	March
For December	$18,300		
For January	22,350	$22,350	
For February		25,950	$25,950
For March			23,400
Total Cash Disbursements for Purchases	$40,650	$48,300	$49,350

Cash Budget—Schedule G

	January	February	March
Beginning cash balance	$9,000	–$ 9,650	–$ 6,950
Cash collections (**Schedule E**)	62,000	73,000	86,000
Total Cash Available	$71,000	$63,350	$79,050
Cash Disbursements			
Inventory Purchases (**Schedule F**)	$40,650	$48,300	$49,350
Operating Expenses (**Schedule C**)	20,500	22,000	22,500
Equip. Pur. (Capital Budget not shown)	19,500	0	0
Total Disbursements	80,650	70,300	71,850
Ending Cash Balance	– 9,650	– 6,950	7,200

A negative cash balance indicates the need to borrow and to revise the budget accordingly.

Exhibit 7.5 *Continued*

Proforma Income Statement—Schedule H

	January	February	March
Sales—**Schedule A**	$70,000	$85,000	$90,000
Cost of Goods Sold—**Schedule B**	−42,000	−51,000	−54,000
Gross Margin	$28,000	$34,000	$36,000
Operating Expenses			
Cash—**Schedule C**	$20,500	$22,000	$22,500
Noncash—**Schedule D**	2,000	2,000	2,000
Operating Expenses	$22,500	$24,000	$24,500
Net Operating Income	$5,500	$10,000	$11,500

Retained Earnings—Schedule G

	January	February	March
Beginning Retained Earnings	$71,300	$76,800	$86,800
Monthly Profit—**Schedule G**	5,500	10,000	11,500
Ending Retained Earnings	$76,800	$86,800	$98,300

Proforma Balance Sheet

	January	February	March
Current Assets			
Cash—**Schedule G**	−$ 9,650	−$ 6,950	$ 7,200
Accts. Receivable—Based on **Schedule E**	56,000	68,000	72,000
Inventory—Based on **Schedule B**	15,300	16,200	9,000
Total Current Assets	$ 61,650	$ 77,250	$ 88,200
Fixed Assets*	217,500	215,500	213,500
Total Assets	$279,150	$292,750	$301,700
Equities			
Accounts Payable—Based on **Schedule F**	$ 22,350	$ 25,950	$ 23,400
Capital Stock	180,000	180,000	180,000
Retained Earnings—**Schedule I**	76,800	86,800	98,300
Total Equities	$279,150	$292,750	$301,700

*Fixed assets consist of beginning fixed assets plus equipment purchased less depreciation.

Coordination

The business plan should now be essentially complete—at least in terms of raw input information.

Following is the **Business Plan Outline** with additional explanatory material. You may want to use this to put the document together. If you are developing another type of plan, modifications may be necessary. When you have gathered all of the paper from the first seven levels, you should see the basis of your plan.

Coordination 0801.doc

Who: When it comes to completing the plan it is usually best to have one person designated to put it into document form. Whoever is so designated should have sufficient clout to require and obtain cooperation to get parts of the plan in as needed.

What: A written document following the outline given earlier. If possible, the basic text portion of the plan should be about 20 pages. The appendices may be as voluminous as necessary to support the plan.

When: The plan should be complete and in the hands of all responsible people 15 to 30 days before it is to become the operative document.

Where: Normally, the plan is completed (put together) in the office environment.

How Long: Finalization should not really be a large problem if the preceding steps have been well followed. Allow at least two weeks, and preferably four, to put the document together.

Business Plan Outline

1. Cover Sheet: With appropriate descriptions
   a. Business name
   b. Business address
   c. Business phone
   d. Principals
   e. Date

2. Sign-up: Signature of all contributors to the plan.

3. Executive Summary: This is what sells someone on reading the remainder of the plan. It should be one or two pages in length and contain the essence of the plan.
   a. For whom is it written?
   b. What is being requested from them?
   c. Why should they be interested in doing it?

4. Table of Contents: Be specific and complete in this area. Some readers may judge the completeness of the plan from the details provided in the table of contents.

5. Major Assumptions: Any planning process creates assumptions upon which certain goals and action plans are premised. Assumptions which are key to the plan should be stated and emergency contingency steps should be formulated for assumptions that may be violated.

6. History Section: If this is a start-up venture, a brief explanation of how the idea (company) came to be is in order at this point. If this is an operating plan, the history section may have the major highlights supplemented with additional details in an appendix.

7. Philosophy: This is taken directly from the work done in **Level 2.** Some people prefer not to publish the philosophy. We suggest you do, as this helps solidify the company around a common set of beliefs.

8. Definition of the Business: It is important that you be able to state succinctly what the business is. This is distinct from what the business does (a listing of functions, products, or services) and is oriented to answering the questions:
   a. What do we do best?
   b. What need does that meet?
   c. Who has that need?

9. Definition of the Market: Markets are composed of buyers and sellers. This section should include some discussion of each. The discussion of buyers could focus on the questions: Who buys and why do they buy? A description of the customer or client base and the factors considered important in the buying decision by them would be appropriate. With respect to sellers, a listing of competitors and a ranking of those competitors with respect to factors held important in the minds of buyers would be helpful. Expectations of changes in market penetration by the company and its competitors should be included.

10. Description of Products or Services: The identified need and the identified market will be accommodated by specific products or services. The description(s) of the products or services should fully explain to the reader why, given the previously stated information, such products or services will be demanded. You may append catalog sheets, pictures, etc.

11. Management Structure: Having described the business, the market, and the product, it is time to indicate who will make things happen. A start-up or financing plan will require more details than will an operating plan. Résumés and other details of the personal backgrounds should be left to an appendix. This section should sell two things: *that you have the right people* and *that they are properly organized.*

12. Strategies, Objectives, Goals, and Tactics: What you intend to accomplish and how. This section will include varying amounts of details based upon the purpose of the plan, but it is important to focus on the *crunch factors*. The detail should be placed in individual appendices. Items to be covered in this section include:

    a. Sales forecasts

    b. Marketing plans

    c. Manufacturing plans

    d. Quality assurance plans

    e. Financial plans

13. Financial Data: The plan is future oriented. Therefore, this section should focus on projections and pro formas. Historical financial information necessary to understanding the plan should be referenced in an appendix. The items to be included are:

    a. Cost–volume–profit analysis

    b. Income projections—pro forma

      • Monthly for planning year

      • Quarterly for second year

      • Annual for third year

c. Cash flow analysis—pro forma
- Monthly for planning year
- Quarterly for second year
- Annual for third year

    d. Break-even analysis

    e. Annual pro forma balance sheets

14. Appendices: These give supporting detail to the content section as well as adding material of interest not otherwise included. If there is proprietary information (patent, research and development, formulas, market research, etc.) that you may wish to control, it would be well to place that information into detachable appendices.

    a. Narrative history of the company

    b. Management structure, additional résumés, organization charts, etc.

    c. Details of objectives, goals, and tactics
- Products and services
- Research and development
- Marketing
- Manufacturing
- Administration
- Finance

    d. Historical financial information (3 to 5 years if possible)

    e. Tax returns (3 to 5 years if possible)

    f. Letters of recommendation or endorsement

    g. Contingency plans

    h. Change process

Well, the plan document is done. Almost!

As surely as you spent time and effort, blood and tears putting this together, some things will change. And when they do, the plan must be flexible enough to recognize the changes and adapt where necessary.

For that reason we have included Exhibit 8.1, Plan Change Process. This is a sample, which you should modify to meet your needs. The page should be kept current so everyone will have an up-to-date version of the plan.

In the final analysis, a plan which does not result in accomplishment is not successful. Therefore, we have also added **Level 9**, Implementation and Follow-up, to bridge the gap between planning and action.

Exhibit 8.1

 0803.doc

Plan Change Process

This plan will be reviewed quarterly by its preparers. The review meeting will be held in the third week after the end of the quarter. The meeting will be called and the location, time, and agenda set by H. Man.
Included in the agenda will be:

1. A review of results obtained
2. A review of assumptions
3. A review of performance vs. plan
4. Suggested changes

Those having suggestions for additional agenda items should submit them at least one week before the meeting.

Changes approved in the meeting will be included in the plan book with changes to appropriate pages.

Date of Change	Pages Changed	Reasons for Change
5/17	12–14	Interest rate changes invalidated basic financial assumptions
7/15	3	New EPA regulation requires change in product formulation

The following pages are hints to help you with the plan presentation. Read through them. Develop a presentation plan.
Good luck!

Business Plan

Major Steps to Acceptance

First Reading. Whether the plan is being presented internally or externally, the first reading is a major step. The plan must offer something that keeps the reader interested. Some things to keep in mind are:

1. Keep it simple.
2. Make it readable (grammatically correct, action oriented, short sentences).
3. Make certain it holds together.
4. Provide an executive summary.

Willingness to Change

1. The plan is a means to accomplish objectives and is not the objective itself.
2. If there is something that needs to be modified, do it before making an in-person presentation.

In-person Presentation. When the plan has passed the first step you will probably be invited to present the plan to appropriate decision makers. This may well be the make-or-break point for the plan. Remember to:

1. Have visual aids for critical segments of the plan
2. Prepare for pointed questions specifically in the areas of:
   a. The ability to make it happen
   b. The adequacy of the research and development behind the product
   c. The validity of the market research
   d. Your understanding of the business

    e. The financial projections and why they will work

    f. Negotiating the lower priorities to achieve the higher ones

Five Pitfalls That Trap Business Plans

1. Erroneous perceptions of the past from:
    a. Inaccurate narrative history
    b. Inadequate financial statements
    c. Ignorance of past mistakes
2. Inadequate forecasts from:
    a. Wrong methodologies
    b. Inadequate internal records
    c. Misunderstanding of effects of externalities
3. Unclear objectives from:
    a. Unstated priorities
    b. Unwritten objectives
    c. Objectives not matching mission
4. Lack of consensus from:
    a. No top-down communication
    b. No top-down push
    c. Varying individual goals
5. Inadequate controls from:
    a. Late or inaccurate reports
    b. Poor analysis
    c. No feedback

10 Ways to Make Sure Your Plan Is a Winner

1. Put it in a loose-leaf binder.
2. Have an established process for change.
3. Be sure everyone has a current copy of the plan.
4. Use the plan as a reporting tool in management meetings.

5. Have all relevant managers sign the plan's sign-up page (back of the first page—gives everyone equity in the plan).

6. Ask the *what if* questions about the assumptions made.

7. Have preliminary responses prepared for probable and/or critical events.

8. Write the plan as a selling document.

9. Target your audience in the executive summary.

10. Keep it short.

Implementation and Follow-up

The experiences of countless thousands of planners have all shown a conclusive proof: *Without the proper follow-up and implementation the probability of any plan being accomplished is very low*. Early in the book, we described the purpose of the plan as being to improve the probability of success. In this section we are going to deal with methods of improving the probability that the plan itself will be successfully implemented and accomplished. **Levels 1 through 8** describe the process of developing a plan and getting the document prepared. In **Level 9**, we will describe the process for helping to get done the things that have been planned.

Implementation and Follow-up 0901.doc

Who: The Facilitator will have the primary responsibility for this. However, it takes the cooperation of all parties to the plan to make it work properly.

What: The product of this process comes in two broadly identified parts: INPUTS and OUTPUTS. The forms contained in this section will assist you with the development of both of these.

When: This process must be initiated before the start of the period for which the plan is operative and continued throughout the planning horizon on whatever basis of regularity you determine is needed (probably not more than monthly nor less than quarterly). These ongoing review procedures should be completed as soon as possible after the completion of the period being reviewed, preferably within not more than two weeks of the end of that period.

Where: These procedures are of the on-site nature.

How Long: The initial input process should not take more than two weeks at the longest. The ongoing review inputs should be completed in a matter of a few days.

As difficult and time consuming as the process of developing a document is, the process of implementing and following through on it is at least equally difficult. It is the implementation and follow through that make the difference between success and failure. Therefore, we will spend some time showing you techniques of improving upon your implementation and follow-through process.

The major task-centered efforts of implementing the plan are handled by the people on the bottom line of the organization chart—the people who have had the least input into the plan and the least communication about the plan. It is important that they be brought into the process as directly as possible and that they clearly understand not only what they are supposed to do but also by when they are to do it and the consequences associated with the result, both positive and negative. They need to understand how what they are doing fits into the overall scheme and why their piece, no matter how small, is important and necessary. This simply requires communication.

In **Level 6** we produced **Individual Accountability and Action Plans** and **Individual Performance Evaluation** sheets. These should be of significant help in assisting employees to understand their responsibilities and how they will be evaluated. In addition, we have provided a sheet entitled **Individual Performance Expectations: Summary of Tactics/Action Steps Assigned** and a related Instructions sheet in Exhibits 9.1 and 9.2. These are used to summarize the assignments for each employee who has any Tactic/Action Steps assigned to them. The sheet identifies which Goal the Step is part of, specifically, what the Step is, by when it is to be done, and how both the employee and the supervisor will know the task has been accomplished.

This process, which should be finished within the two weeks immediately preceding the start of the plan period, will remind supervisors as well as employees of the work that is to be accomplished, by when, and by whom. By refreshing everyone's memories, since the planning process may have otherwise been completed weeks or months before, you will greatly improve the probability of success.

Both the employees and the supervisors will then have **Summary** sheets to which they may return at the end of each quarter to evaluate the accomplishment of specific tasks, specific individuals, and specific goals. Supervisors will want to use the **Individual Performance Evalua-**

EXHIBIT 9.1   0903.xls

Individual Performance Expectations—Summary of Tactics/Action Steps Assigned

Name: <u>M. Employee</u>   Page <u>1</u> of <u>1</u>
Department: <u>Marketing</u>   Acknowledged by: _____
                                                Date: _____

Goal ID #	Tactic/Action Step Assigned	Completion Date	Evidence of Completion
MKT 1.01	Develop market survey of Northwest Territory	5/15/9X	Survey OK by MM
MKT 1.01	Pretest survey	6/15/9X	Pretest results to MM
MKT 3.04	Visit each salesman in N.W. territory at least once	12/30/9X	Visitation reports to MM

tion sheets quarterly, semiannually, or at least annually as a scorecard for employees' performances.

Having started "from the bottom" with an evaluation of task and individual performance, we now begin to aggregate that evaluation across Goals and Objectives.

In **Level 4**, we listed the characteristics of well-stated Objectives and Goals. These are:

- Specific
- Measurable
- Actionable
- Relevant
- Monitorable

- Clear
- Concise
- Consistent
- Motivating
- Divisible

- Positive
- Reasonable
- Inclusive
- Timebound
- Congruent

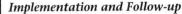

Exhibit 9.2

Individual Performance Expectations—Instructions

12/20/9X
Due Date

Plan Facilitator
Planning Facilitator

Each Responsible Manager should complete an Individual Performance Expectations (IPE) sheet for each employee to whom one or more Action Steps has been assigned for one or more Goals.

Primarily, the IPE sheet is a consolidation of information from the Goal Action Plan Sheets. It is intended to help the employee and manager understand and track the Tactics/Action Steps for which an individual is responsible.

As the Responsible Manager, you should:

1. Complete the Name and Department information.
2. List the Goal ID #, the Tactic/Action Step Assigned, the Completion Date by which this step should be done, and the Evidence of Completion for *each* item assigned to this person. This information can be taken from the Goal Action Plan Sheets.
3. Complete the "Page __ of __" indicators for each page for each person.
4. Give a copy of each Employee's IPE to that Employee and discuss the expectations.
5. Have each employee sign and date (Acknowledged by and Date) the original IPE and return it to you. The employee should retain a copy.
6. Keep a copy and give the original to the Planning Facilitator by the Due Date.
7. At least quarterly, review the IPE sheets with each of your employees as a part of the plan progress review.

We will focus our attention on two of those characteristics at this time—Measurable and Monitorable.

Of course, all of the Objectives should be important to the success of the company. However, they may not all be equally important. Therefore, you may want to have the Senior Managers who, in **Level 4**, helped to formulate the Objectives to provide input into the development of weights to be assigned to those Objectives. Or, you (with or without assistance from anyone else) may choose weights for the Objectives.

If you want to have the input from others, you may choose to use the **Corporate Objectives Weighting Sheet** and related Instructions in Exhibits 9.3 and 9.4. If so, you will need to do the following:

- Complete the Due Date by which you want the form returned to you, the FYE (Fiscal Year Ending) designation which the plan covers, and your name (Planning Facilitator).

- Assign identification numbers to the Corporate Objectives (if this has not already been done as a part of **Level 5** when the Planning Unit Goal Sheets were developed) and put the numbers and a statement of the Objectives in Columns 1 and 2 of the Corporate Objectives Weighting Sheet. Leave Column 3 to be completed by the respondents.

- Complete the Due Date, FYE, and Planning Coordinator blanks on the Corporate Objectives Weighting Sheet Instructions page.

- Distribute these sheets to all from whom you wish to have response.

- When you receive the responses, make a final determination of the appropriate weight to be assigned to each Objective.

EXHIBIT 9.3 _____ 0904.xls

Corporate Objectives

WEIGHTING SHEET
FYE: ___199X___

December 17, 199X
Due Date

Plan Facilitator
Planning Facilitator

Col. 1	Col. 2	Col. 3
Number	**Statement of the Objective**	**Weight**
1	Introduce X-Tron into three market territories by May 30, 199X	
2	Net income before tax of $2.3 MM for fiscal 199X	
3	Enhance each employee's job satisfaction skills	
XXXXXXXXX	XXXXXXXXXXXXXXXXXXXXXXXXXXXXXXXX	100%

EXHIBIT 9.4

Corporate Objectives

WEIGHTING SHEET

FYE: ___199X___

INSTRUCTIONS

December 17, 199X

Due Date

Plan Facilitator

Planning Facilitator

Attached is the Corporate Objectives Weighting Sheet. Columns 1 and 2 have been completed for you.

Please review these Objectives, as previously established by Senior Management, and assign weights (portion of 100%) to each one that reflects your interpretation of the relative importance of that objective. You may feel that all should be evenly weighted. Or, you may wish to assign heavier weights to some than others.

NOTE: The total of all assigned weights must be 100%.

This information will be aggregated and final weights will be assigned to the Objectives.

In order to get the necessary documentation for specific evaluation of the accomplishment at the Departmental Goal level, you will require additional input from the Responsible Managers.

For each Responsible Manager develop a **Goal Listing Sheet** such as the one in Exhibit 9.5. These Goals are simply consolidations of the Goals submitted on the **Planning Unit Goal Sheets** from **Level 5** with an identification added. It provides two things: a final check on the accuracy of the Goal statement as you have it and a means of referencing that Goal without having to state it each time. Each Goal should have a unique designation that identifies it with both the Objective which it supports and the Department which has committed to its completion. Therefore, a designation such as ACC1.01 may be appropriate. This would identify ACCounting as the department, **1.** as the Objective, and **01** as Accounting's first Goal related to this Objective. (ACC03.05 would indicate that Accounting has established at least five Goals it will accomplish relative to Objective 3). Designations such as **MKT, MFG,** and **ADM** could be used for Marketing, Manufacturing, and Administration.

EXHIBIT 9.5 0905.xls

Goal Listing Sheet

FYE: ___199X___

Manager: <u>Responsible Person</u>

Goal Identification #	Goal Statement
ACC1.01	Statement of Goal 1 for Objective 1
ACC1.02	Statement of Goal 2 for Objective 1
ACC2.01	Statement of only Goal for Objective 2
ACC3.01	Statement of only Goal for Objective 3

Also, for each Responsible Manager, develop the **Goal Weighting and Progress Chart** and related Instructions as shown in Exhibits 9.6 and 9.7. For the initial information period, you will complete the following:

- FYE (both forms)
- Planning Facilitator (both forms)
- Responsible Person (Goal Weighting and Progress Chart)
- Columns 1, 2, and 3 as appropriate from your weighting of the Corporate Objectives and the Goal Listing Sheet for this manager.

Before doing the next two steps, make four (4) copies of each **Goal Weighting and Progress Chart** as completed so far. Then proceed with the next two steps on only the original from which you made the copies.

EXHIBIT 9.6

 0906.xls

Goal Weighting and Progress Chart

FYE: ___199X___

December 21, 199X
Due Date

Plan Facilitator
Planning Facilitator

Please complete the indicated columns and return to the Planning Facilitator on or before the Due Date.

Responsible Person: *Responsible Person*

Columns to be Completed

| 1 | 2 | 3 | 4 | 5 | 6 | 7 | 8 | 9 | 10 | 11 | 12 |

Corp. Obj. No.	Weight to Objective	Goal No.	Weight to Goal	Exp. 1st Qtr.	Act. 1st Qtr.	Exp. 2nd Qtr.	Act. 2nd Qtr.	Exp. 3rd Qtr.	Act. 3rd Qtr.	Exp. 4th Qtr.	Act. 4th Qtr.
				Cumulative Completion Percentage*							
1	30%	ACC 1.01								100%	
1	30%	ACC 1.02								100%	
2	50%	ACC 2.01								100%	
3	20%	ACC 3.01								100%	
										100%	
										100%	
										100%	
										100%	
										100%	
										100%	
										100%	
										100%	
										100%	
										100%	
XX	XX	XX	100%	XX	XX	XX	XX	XX	XX	XX	XX
Col 1	Col 2	Col 3	Col 4	Col 5	Col 6	Col 7	Col 8	Col 9	Col 10	Col 11	Col 12

*Exp = Expected at beginning of plan year *Act = Actual at end of quarter
Expected columns to be completed fully. Actual columns to be completed at the end of the quarter.

EXHIBIT 9.7

Goal Weighting and Progress Chart

FYE: ___199X___

INSTRUCTIONS

December 21, 199X _____   Plan Facilitator _____
Due Date   Planning Facilitator

You have received a summary of all the Goals for your responsibility area with a Goal Identification number assigned and a Goal Weighting and Progress Chart listing all your Goals by Identification Number. If this is not so, please contact the Planning Facilitator immediately.

The Goal Listing Sheet is a summary of the Goals you have established for yourself and your responsibility area. It is for your information.

Goal Weighting and Progress Chart Instructions:

1. Columns 1, 2, and 3 have been completed for you.
2. Looking at your Goal Listing Sheet and considering the weight assigned to the related Corporate Objectives, (Col. 2), assign a weight (portion of 100%) to each listed Goal. Place the assigned weight in Col. 4 beside each Goal number (Col. 3).
3. Note that the sum of all Goal Weights for your Department must be 100%.
4. For each listed Goal, complete Cols. 5, 7, and 9 with the **cumulative** percentage of that Goal which you plan to attain by the end of the indicated quarter. Note that Col. 11 already indicates the planned cumulative percentage completion at the end of the 4th quarter to be 100%.
5. The same sheet will be used at the end of each quarter for you to record the Actual Completion of each Goal. However, at this time, Cols. 6, 8, 10, and 12 should be left blank.
6. When you have completed the above, make a copy of this sheet for your records and return the original to the Planning Facilitator by the Due Date above.

- Due Date (both forms)
- Columns to be Completed—check columns 4, 5, 7, 9 (Goal Weighting and Progress Chart)

You will note that Instruction 5 indicates that the same (or similar) sheets will be used at the end of each quarter to allow the Responsible Managers to record their perceived Actual Accomplishments (in Columns 6, 8, 10, and 12, respectively).

Copies of the **Goal Weighting and Progress Chart** and related Instructions for the evaluations at the end of each quarter are also included. If you will make four (4) copies of the first **Goal Weighting and Progress Chart** BEFORE you fill in the Due Date or the Columns to be Completed you will be able to use these for the quarter-end follow through and will eliminate some duplication of effort.

Exhibit 9.8 shows a copy of the **Goal Weighting and Progress Chart** form as it might look when returned before the beginning of the plan period.

The **Goal Weighting and Progress Chart** in Exhibit 9.9 is to be used at the end of the first quarter to receive information about the completion of tasks. If you made copies of the original **Goal Progress and Weighting Chart**, use one of those copies. If not, you will need to complete sheets for each Responsible Manager with all previously received information filled in. The Instruction sheets for each quarter shown in Exhibit 9.10 have been developed on the assumption that you made copies of the original sheet before the beginning of the plan period.

Exhibit 9.11 through Exhibit 9.13 are provided for those who prefer a mathematical model for aggregating results and showing those results as a single quantity—deviation from plan. Many find such a process too burdensome and without cost–benefit merit. Others believe a single quantitative measure is a better motivational tool.

On the following pages you will see output developed and used in consultations with clients. You may want to use this as a model to create a format you can use as the basis for developing your own analysis spreadsheet.

Original plan input for: SAMPLE

This plan is composed of 4 components or GOALS and is expected to take 4 periods to complete.

Listed below are the WEIGHTS (percentage of total plan) that were assigned to the individual components or GOALS.

GOAL	WEIGHT	EXPECTED COMPLETION BY QUARTER			
		Q1	Q2	Q3	Q4
ACC1.01	25%	50%	70%	90%	100%
ACC1.02	10%	25%	50%	75%	100%
ACC2.01	50%	50%	100%	100%	100%
ACC3.01	15%	30%	60%	100%	100%
TOTAL PROGRESS		45%	82%	95%	100%

Exhibit 9.8

Goal Weighting and Progress Chart

FYE: __199X__

December 21, 199X
Due Date

Plan Facilitator
Planning Facilitator

Please complete the indicated columns and return to the Planning Facilitator on or before the Due Date.

Responsible Person: _Responsible Person_

Columns to be Completed
| 1 | 2 | 3 | 4 | 5 | 6 | 7 | 8 | 9 | 10 | 11 | 12 |

Corp. Obj. No.	Weight to Objective	Goal No.	Weight to Goal	Exp. 1st Qtr.	Act. 1st Qtr.	Exp. 2nd Qtr.	Act. 2nd Qtr.	Exp. 3rd Qtr.	Act. 3rd Qtr.	Exp. 4th Qtr.	Act. 4th Qtr.
1	30%	ACC 1.01	25%	50%		70%		90%		100%	
1	30%	ACC 1.02	10%	25%		50%		75%		100%	
2	50%	ACC 2.01	50%	50%		100%		100%		100%	
3	20%	ACC 3.01	15%	30%		60%		100%		100%	
										100%	
										100%	
										100%	
										100%	
										100%	
										100%	
										100%	
										100%	
										100%	
										100%	
XX	XX	XX	100%	XX	XX	XX	XX	XX	XX	XX	XX
Col 1	Col 2	Col 3	Col 4	Col 5	Col 6	Col 7	Col 8	Col 9	Col 10	Col 11	Col 12

*Exp = Expected at beginning of plan year *Act = Actual at end of quarter
Expected columns to be completed fully. Actual columns to be completed at the end of the quarter.

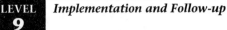
EXHIBIT 9.9

Goal Weighting and Progress Chart

FYE: ___199X___

April 5, 199X
Due Date

Plan Facilitator
Planning Facilitator

Please complete the indicated columns and return to the Planning Facilitator on or before the Due Date.

Responsible Person: _Responsible Person_

Columns to be Completed
| 1 | 2 | 3 | 4 | 5 | 6 | 7 | 8 | 9 | 10 | 11 | 12 |

Corp. Obj. No.	Weight to Objective	Goal No.	Weight to Goal	Exp. 1st Qtr.	Act. 1st Qtr.	Exp. 2nd Qtr.	Act. 2nd Qtr.	Exp. 3rd Qtr.	Act. 3rd Qtr.	Exp. 4th Qtr.	Act. 4th Qtr.
				Cumulative Completion Percentage*							
1	30%	ACC 1.01	25%	50%		70%		90%		100%	
1	30%	ACC 1.02	10%	25%		50%		75%		100%	
2	50%	ACC 2.01	50%	50%		100%		100%		100%	
3	20%	ACC 3.01	15%	30%		60%		100%		100%	
										100%	
										100%	
										100%	
										100%	
										100%	
										100%	
										100%	
										100%	
										100%	
										100%	
XX	XX	XX	100%	XX	XX	XX	XX	XX	XX	XX	XX
Col 1	Col 2	Col 3	Col 4	Col 5	Col 6	Col 7	Col 8	Col 9	Col 10	Col 11	Col 12

*Exp = Expected at beginning of plan year *Act = Actual at end of quarter
Expected columns to be completed fully. Actual columns to be completed at the end of the quarter.

Exhibit 9.10

Goal Weighting and Progress Chart

FYE: ___199X___

First Quarter Instructions

April 5, 199X   Plan Facilitator
Due Date   Planning Facilitator

Attached is a copy of a Goal Weighting and Progress Chart for you. Columns 1, 2, 3, 4, 5, 7, 9, and 11 are completed.

You are to complete Column 6 which is your evaluation of the Actual Completion Percentage on each of your Goals as of the end of Quarter 1.

Return the Goal Weighting and Progress Chart sheet to the Planning Facilitator by the Due Date.

(continued)

EXHIBIT **9.10** *Continued*

Goal Weighting and Progress Chart

FYE: ___199X___

Second Quarter Instructions

Due Date   Planning Facilitator

Attached is a copy of a Goal Weighting and Progress Chart for you. Columns 1, 2, 3, 4, 5, 6, 7, 9, and 11 are completed.

You are to complete Column 8 which is your evaluation of the Actual Completion Percentage on each of your Goals as of the end of Quarter 2.

Return the Goal Weighting and Progress Chart sheet to the Planning Facilitator by the Due Date.

EXHIBIT **9.10** *Continued*

Goal Weighting and Progress Chart

FYE: __199X__

Third Quarter Instructions

Due Date   Planning Facilitator

Attached is a copy of a Goal Weighting and Progress Chart for you. Columns 1, 2, 3, 4, 5, 6, 7, 8, 9, and 11 are completed.

You are to complete Column 10 which is your evaluation of the Actual Completion Percentage on each of your Goals as of the end of Quarter 3.

Return the Goal Weighting and Progress Chart sheet to the Planning Facilitator by the Due Date.

(continued)

EXHIBIT **9.10** *Continued*

Goal Weighting and Progress Chart

FYE: ___199X___

Fourth Quarter Instructions

Due Date   Planning Facilitator

Attached is a copy of a Goal Weighting and Progress Chart for you. Columns 1, 2, 3, 4, 5, 6, 7, 8, 9, 10, and 11 are completed.

You are to complete Column 12 which is your evaluation of the Actual Completion Percentage on each of your Goals as of the year-end.

Return the Goal Weighting and Progress Chart sheet to the Planning Facilitator by the Due Date.

The input for this program is taken from the **Goal Weighting and Progress Chart** form on the previous pages. The inputs are repeated on the printout so that they can be checked against the form for accuracy. The TOTAL PROGRESS calculation at the bottom is the summation of the multiplication of the WEIGHT times EXPECTED COMPLETION BY QUARTER.

For example, TOTAL PROGRESS Q1 is (.25 * .50) + (.1 * .25) + (.5 * .5) + (.15 * .3) or .125 + .025 + .25 + .045 = .445 or .45 rounded. That is, based upon the weights and the expectations, Accounting expects to achieve 45% of the total significance of its plan in the first quarter. By the end of the second quarter it expects to be 82% complete.

A copy of the **Goal Weighting and Progress Chart—First Quarter** form as it might look when returned at the end of the first quarter is shown in Exhibit 9.11.

The Quarter 1 input is solicited from each Responsible Manager as soon as possible after the end of the quarter. The completed form for Quarter 1 is the source of the information put into the program. This indicates that Accounting has made significant progress on three of its four goals but no progress as yet on the fourth.

Quarter 1 input for: SAMPLE

		ACTUAL COMPLETION BY QUARTER			
GOAL	WEIGHT	Q1	Q2	Q3	Q4
ACC1.01	25%	45%	0%	0%	0%
ACC1.02	10%	35%	0%	0%	0%
ACC2.01	50%	75%	0%	0%	0%
ACC3.01	15%	0%	0%	0%	0%
TOTAL PROGRESS		52%	0%	0%	0%

The first table on the following page (Quarter 1 output for: SAMPLE) restates previous information and calculates PERCENT CHANGE. The PERCENT CHANGE column is calculated as follows:

(Actual – Expected) / Expected

For ACC1.01 that is (.45 – .5) / .5 or –.05 / .5 = –.10 which is the –10% PERCENT CHANGE.

The second table on that page provides an additional breakdown of information. The WEIGHTED EXPECTED and WEIGHTED ACTUAL columns are the multiplications of the WEIGHT and the respective

Exhibit 9.11

Goal Weighting and Progress Chart

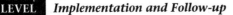

FYE: ___199X___

April 5, 199X
Due Date

Plan Facilitator
Planning Facilitator

Please complete the indicated columns and return to the Planning Facilitator on or before the Due Date.

Columns to be Completed

Responsible Person: *Responsible Person* | 1 | 2 | 3 | 4 | 5 | 6 | 7 | 8 | 9 | 10 | 11 | 12 |

| Corp. Obj. No. | Weight to Objective | Goal No. | Weight to Goal | Cumulative Completion Percentage* | | | | | | | |
				Exp. 1st Qtr.	Act. 1st Qtr.	Exp. 2nd Qtr.	Act. 2nd Qtr.	Exp. 3rd Qtr.	Act. 3rd Qtr.	Exp. 4th Qtr.	Act. 4th Qtr.
1	30%	ACC 1.01	25%	50%	45%	70%		90%		100%	
1	30%	ACC 1.02	10%	25%	35%	50%		75%		100%	
2	50%	ACC 2.01	50%	50%	75%	100%		100%		100%	
3	20%	ACC 3.01	15%	30%	0%	60%		100%		100%	
										100%	
										100%	
										100%	
										100%	
										100%	
										100%	
										100%	
										100%	
										100%	
										100%	
XX	XX	XX	100%	XX	XX	XX	XX	XX	XX	XX	XX
Col 1	Col 2	Col 3	Col 4	Col 5	Col 6	Col 7	Col 8	Col 9	Col 10	Col 11	Col 12

*Exp = Expected at beginning of plan year *Act = Actual at end of quarter
Expected columns to be completed fully. Actual columns to be completed at the end of the quarter.

EXPECTED and ACTUAL columns above. In each case, the TOTAL simply sums the column.

The VARIANCE column is the WEIGHTED ACTUAL column minus the WEIGHTED EXPECTED column. This explains the difference in weighted percentage points. That is, ACC1.01 was EXPECTED to have 12.5 weighted percentage points completed but had ACTUAL weighted percentage points completed of 11.25. Therefore, it was 1.25 weighted percentage points behind.

In all, the WEIGHTED ACTUAL is 7.75 weighted percentage points more than the WEIGHTED EXPECTED (52.25% – 44.5%).

The VARIANCE FROM PLAN EXPLAINED is the VARIANCE column divided by the WEIGHTED EXPECTED TOTAL. That is, ACC1.01 explains 2.81% negative variance, ACC1.02 explains 2.25% positive variance, etc. In all, for the quarter the plan is 17.42% ahead (7.75% / 44.5%).

From this analysis, the reviewer can see that Accounting is making excellent progress. However, just to say that we are 17.42% ahead of plan would be misleading. It may also be important to note that different Goals are not being evenly met. The failure to make timely progress on these goals may indicate they will not be completed in the year or it may foretell of difficulties for other departments which are relying on the completion of these Goals as a basis for work they must do.

This same type of analysis will be done every quarter so that the departments can assess their accomplishments and the overall plan success can be tracked. This overall tracking is a more difficult job.

Quarter 1 output for: SAMPLE

GOAL	WEIGHT	EXPECTED Q1	ACTUAL Q1	PERCENT CHANGE
ACC1.01	25%	50%	45%	–10%
ACC1.02	10%	25%	35%	40%
ACC2.01	50%	50%	75%	50%
ACC3.01	15%	30%	0%	–100%

Quarter 1 output for: SAMPLE

GOAL	WEIGHTED EXPECTED	WEIGHTED ACTUAL	VARIANCE	VARIANCE FROM PLAN EXPLAINED
ACC1.01	12.50%	11.25%	–1.25%	–2.81%
ACC1.02	2.50%	3.50%	1.00%	2.25%
ACC2.01	25.00%	37.50%	12.50%	28.09%
ACC3.01	4.50%	0.00%	–4.50%	–10.11%
TOTAL	44.50%	52.25%	7.75%	17.42%

The SAMPLE graphic in Exhibit 9.12 simply puts into picture format some of the information gathered or created so far. The EXPECTED bars (Q1 left, Q2, Q3, and Q4) are from the Original plan input for: SAMPLE, on page 128, where the TOTAL PROGRESS row shows 45%, 82%, 95%, and 100%. The Q1 Actual bar is from Quarter 1 output for: SAMPLE, Weighted Actual Total above.

This graphic can be added onto each quarter to give a cumulative picture of accomplishment.

At year-end, the goals for all departments are listed by Objective along with both the WEIGHTED EXPECTED COMPLETION and the WEIGHTED ACTUAL COMPLETION. These are then summed to give the TOTAL WEIGHTED EXPECTED COMPLETION and the TOTAL WEIGHTED ACTUAL COMPLETION by Objective.

Then, the RELATIVE COMPLETION OF ALL GOALS FOR OBJECTIVE is calculated by dividing the TOTAL WEIGHTED ACTUAL COMPLETION by the TOTAL WEIGHTED EXPECTED COMPLETION.

Example for Objective 1: SAMPLE

GOALS	WEIGHTED EXPECTED COMPLETION	WEIGHTED ACTUAL COMPLETION
ACC1.01	25.00%	20.00%
ACC1.01	10.00%	10.00%
ADM1.01	50.00%	45.00%
MKT1.01	10.00%	9.00%
MFG1.01	25.00%	25.00%
MFG1.02	30.00%	15.00%

RELATIVE COMPLETION OF ALL GOALS
FOR OBJECTIVE 1: 82.67%.

Exhibit 9.13 takes the information from the WEIGHT column and the YEAR-END WEIGHTED COMPLETION column. Since all Objectives are expected to be 100% completed, the WEIGHT column represents YEAR-END WEIGHTED COMPLETION.

The WEIGHT for each Objective is multiplied by the RELATIVE COMPLETION to produce the YEAR-END WEIGHTED COMPLETION. Obviously, if all goals for all Objectives are met, the TOTAL YEAR-END WEIGHTED COMPLETION will be 100%. The VARIANCE is the difference between the WEIGHT and the YEAR-END EXPECTED COMPLETION.

EXHIBIT **9.12**

Sample—Comparison of Expected to Actual

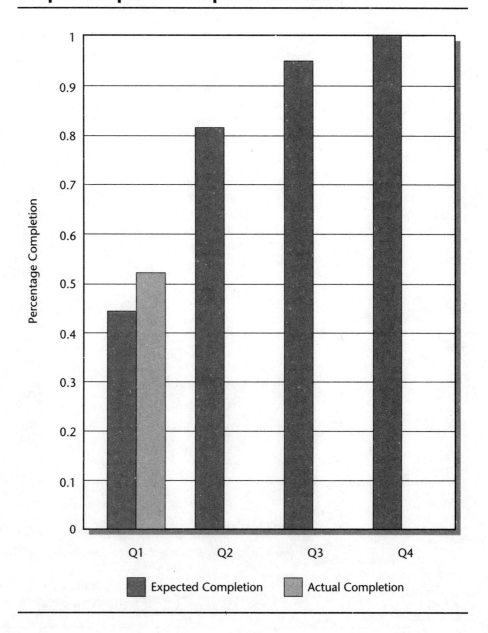

EXHIBIT 9.13

Sample—Comparison of Expected to Actual

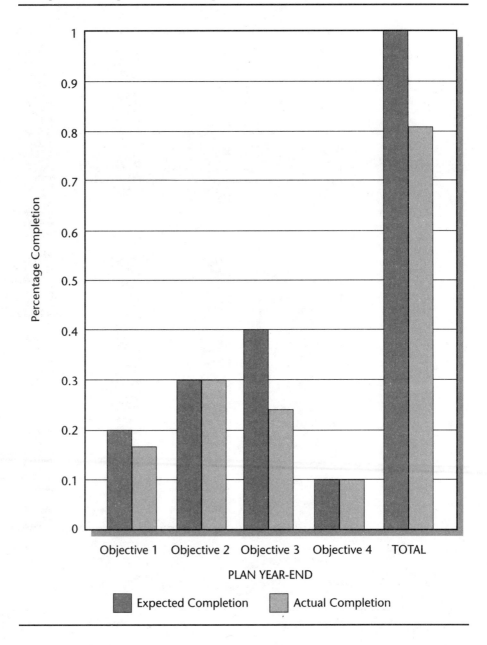

OBJECTIVE	WEIGHT	RELATIVE COMPLETION	YEAR-END WEIGHTED COMPLETION	VARIANCE
OBJECTIVE 1	20.00%	82.67%	16.53%	–3.47%
OBJECTIVE 2	30.00%	100.00%	30.00%	0.00%
OBJECTIVE 3	40.00%	60.00%	24.00%	–16.00%
OBJECTIVE 4	10.00%	100.00%	10.00%	0.00%
TOTAL	100.00%		80.53%	–19.47%

There is no way to guarantee the success of any plan. However, without appropriate implementation and follow through you can be almost certain of failure. The forms and instructions in this section will be of great value to you in your implementation and follow-through process. Communication and evaluation should be a daily process—not just a quarterly one.

As with all of the suggestions throughout this book, the ideas expressed and the methods used in this section do work. You may, however, need to adapt and modify them to fit your organization. There really is such a thing as organizational culture, and the planning process must be made to fit within it.

Planning is important. Planning is vital. Planning is even fun. But making it happen is what it is all about. Using the suggestions in this section will help you make it happen.

Conclusion

The manner in which the business plan is positioned is sometimes as important as the content of the plan. If the plan is dismissed by senior decision makers for reasons other than the viability of the content, it really does not matter how good the content is. Positioning can make or break the possibility of having the plan accepted. That positioning comes in five parts: Selling the Plan Concept, Communication While the Plan Is Being Developed, Delivery of the Written Document, The In-Person Presentation, and, in the long-run, Results of Plan Implementation.

Selling the Plan Concept

If the senior decision makers are not convinced of the need for a plan or if they have a different concept of what the plan is supposed to accomplish than you do, you may have significant difficulty selling the final plan or, even worse, being rewarded when the plan is accomplished. It is imperative that you come to agreement about why you need a plan and what the plan will accomplish. In most organizations, this will be done through a combination of informal conversations, meetings, and written documents.

There are at least five excellent reasons for doing a plan (other than being required to do so by the boss or external forces):

1. To develop a management framework against which all major decisions, including resource allocations, can be made
2. As a means of establishing the standard against which actual performance will be measured
3. As a means of motivating and rewarding managers and other contributors

4. As a tool for educating personnel concerning the business
5. As a means of communicating expectations and demonstrating results

It is important that you sell all five of these benefits from the beginning. Before the plan development is even begun, you should make the effort to lay this groundwork with all involved parties and to document the agreement as to what the reasonable expectations from the planning process are. This will most likely culminate in a memo or other written document circulated to all participating parties.

You may wish to refer to the Introduction of this book where sections entitled **Using This Process, Frequently Asked Questions (with Answers) about Business Planning,** and **Elements of a Good Plan** are presented. This information will be useful in establishing common grounds of expectations and selling the concept. Read these sections again carefully before you deliver the written document and/or make an in-person presentation. You may find information of value to you for both of these cases as well.

Communication While the Plan Is Being Developed

Once you have sold the idea of planning and of a formal plan, it is also important to keep everyone informed as the plan is being developed. If the process takes several months, as it often does, some people "fall out of the loop" and lose track of what has happened. You should develop a schedule of anticipated events, dates, and participants (see *Business Plan Coordination Time Chart* in the **Introduction**) to be given to everyone at the beginning of the process. Then, stay on the schedule as much as possible and communicate to all interested parties before and after each milestone point.

Eliminating surprises as to the outcomes of the planning effort and making it as easy as possible for people to participate and have success is very valuable in selling the final outcome.

Delivery of the Written Document

At the end of **Level 8** we discussed **Major Steps to Acceptance** and **10 Ways to Make Sure Your Plan Is a Winner.** We will elaborate on some of the points abbreviated there.

The plan is a selling document. It is used to "sell" senior decision-makers, bankers, coworkers, and everyone to whom it is presented. Always keep in mind that its purpose is to sell. Construct and present it accordingly. It should be attractively packaged without detracting from its purpose. It should be short. Whenever possible, condense the basic text of the plan to 20 or fewer pages.

When the text is kept to 20 pages or less, you have an excellent chance of having it read. Almost as important, you have an excellent chance of having it read in one seating so that the continuity comes through. As the size of the document increases, the probability of having it read in its entirety diminishes. Presenting the document in two parts may help. The basic text of the plan can be in one volume and the appendix in another. This makes the size of the "reading" portion less ominous.

Make certain the writing is grammatically correct, sentences and paragraphs are short, and the verbs are active. While the reader probably is familiar with the business already, do not assume too much. Give enough background to be certain that any reader can follow the thoughts logically but do not ramble. One way to focus attention and avoid rambling is to have a new subheading about every half page. This virtually forces you to isolate on a point, make it, and move on.

It may be that you will want or need to prepare more than one version of the written document if you have significantly different audiences with different needs or interests. Since this is a selling document it must be written to a target audience. The level of detail may vary drastically for internal users and external users. Proprietary information may be left in the internal version but abstracted or omitted from the version given to bankers or other outside users.

Perhaps the most important pages are those labeled Executive Summary. Although these pages are usually written last, they are presented first and often serve as the "Five-Minute Cut." Some decision makers will read only the Executive Summary (which takes about five minutes) and will form most of their decision on that basis. Therefore, these few pages must not only present the whole story in a nutshell but also sell the plan at the same time. Often, it takes as long to write these few pages as it does to write the rest of the plan because it is very difficult to say all that must be said in this brief space.

The In-Person Presentation

There are different schools of thought concerning the order of the in-person presentation and the delivery of the written document. Some feel that an in-person presentation after a decision maker has a written document is anticlimactic. Therefore, they wait until after the in-person presentation to provide the written document. Others feel that an in-person presentation is more effective when the listener has read the document, is already familiar with the subject and can ask informed questions.

From our point of view either of these will work. What is usually a problem is delivering the written document and making the in-person presentation at the same time. Often, this means the decision maker is trying to read the document as the presentation is being made. We prefer the decision maker to have read the document before the in-person presentation is made. If that is not to be the case, we prefer not to give the written document until after the presentation has been concluded.

The in-person presentation should be complete with all the normal sales tools. Slides, transparencies, videos, computer graphics, or whatever you would use to make a sale (or which the decision maker would normally expect in a sales presentation) should be prepared and used. The presentation should be not more than 30 minutes long, and you may want to ask that questions be reserved to the end in order that the continuity of the plan can be presented, unbroken.

Leave ample time for questions and be prepared for very pointed ones. This may require that you practice this presentation with other audiences before you get to your "audience of significance."

Perhaps the most important part of both the written and the in-person presentations is this: State precisely what it is you want from the decision maker, why they should give it to you, and what they get back in return.

Results of Plan Implementation

Once you have the go ahead to implement the plan, the feedback from plan accomplishment is very important for the probability of getting future plans accepted. Nothing sells planning like success. However, feedback must not be colored to hide problems but must be forthright and revealing. In **Level 9** we discussed **Implementation and Follow-up.** There are several forms provided to help you gather and present timely feedback and to control the process. Whether you adopt these forms "as is" or adapt them to your specific needs, be certain to have a process ready to go at the beginning of the planning period and use it routinely (monthly or quarterly) to provide the kind of information flow that keeps everyone on target and informed.

Appendix

Business Planning Terms

Vision.   The view of the future of the organization, which stresses what the visionary wants the organization to become. It is the integration and synthesis of information with dreams.

Philosophy.   The set of basic beliefs which establishes the parameters for the business and its personnel. It is a statement of what we do and what we do not do.

- Why are we in business?
- How do we do business?
- What do we do and not do as a business?

Mission.   The primary focus of the business which answers the question,

- What business are we in?

Status.   An assessment of the present position which answers the question,

- Where are we?

Strategy.   A method or course of action for dealing with competitors. It can be either proactive or reactive.

- Who else is in this business?
- How do we relate to them?

Objective.   An aim or end of an action; results to be accomplished. For the *business as a whole* it answers the question,

- Where does the business want to go?

Goal.   A point toward which a planning unit strives; a step toward accomplishing an objective. For the *planning unit* it answers the question,

- Where does the planning unit want to go?

Tactic.   Methods of using resources to reach goals. It helps to answer the question,

- How do we get there?

Projection.   A quantitative estimate of the results expected from using various tactics, particularly those we expect to employ.

- What will it look like when we do get there?

Budget.   The quantification of the plan. It should show expected benefits (in financial terms) and the costs needed to achieve those benefits. It should be driven by the plan rather than driving the plan.

Elements

0001.doc

Vision: _____

_____

_____

Commitment: _____

_____

_____

Timelines: _____

_____

_____

Phasing: _____

_____

_____

Contingencies: _____

_____

_____

Reporting: _____

_____

_____

Change: _____

_____

_____

Business Plan Outline

1. Cover Sheet
   a. Company name and/or logo
   b. Business plan and year
   c. Names (perhaps with phone numbers)

2. Sign-up Page

3. Executive Summary
   a. Two pages
   b. What's in it for the reader?
   c. How many different readers?

4. Table of Contents
   a. Make it detailed enough to be useful
   b. Should be about one heading per page of text

5. Major Assumptions
   a. Economy
   b. Suppliers
   c. Consumers
   d. Competition

6. History Section
   a. Two pages maximum
   b. Focus on relationship to plans
   c. Major events

7. Philosophy

8. Definition of the Business
   a. Usually less than one page
   b. What business(es) are we in?
   c. What is the glue holding us together?

9. Definition of the Market
   a. Consider buyers and sellers
   b. Can use strategic factors analysis to help describe sellers (competitive analysis)
   c. Describe buyers demographically, psychographically, and by distribution channel

10. Description of Products or Services
    a. Most emphasis on new ones
    b. Advertising information sometimes helpful
    c. No catalogs

11. Management Structure
    a. Show that you have the right people
    b. Quarter-page résumés
    c. Relate résumés to goals

12. Strategies, Objectives, Goals, and Tactics
    a. Longest section of the plan
    b. Strategies lead to objectives
    c. Do not forget operational objectives
    d. Objectives lead to goals
    e. Format to reduce writing and ease reading

13. Financial Data
    a. This is the plan translated to dollars
    b. Budgets
       —Capital items
       —Cash flow
       —Revenue and expense
    c. Cost–volume–profit analysis

14. Appendices
    a. Supporting detail
    b. Making it work
    c. Not a dumping ground for superfluous pages

Facilitator's Checklist

0002.doc

Meeting Checklist

Facility Name _____

Address _____

Phone _____

Facility Contact Person _____

Off-hours Contact Person _____

Limo: Phone _____ Cost _____

Car Rental On-site _____

Recreation Available _____ Cost _____

Directions to Facility (if necessary)

_____

_____

Meeting Room Name or Number _____

_____ Ease of Access	_____ Walls Okay for Tape	_____ Rest Rooms Accessible
_____ Noise Level	_____ Windows Covered	_____ Out-of-Room Phone
_____ Visual Distractions	_____ Chairs Comfortable	_____ Break Service Specified
	_____ Table(s) Substantial	

Dining Room Name or Number _____

_____ Size Appropriate	_____ Buffets	_____ Adequate Servers
_____ Separation from Meeting Room	_____ Menu Checked	

Equipment

_____ Flip Charts and Stands (with backs)	_____ Note Pads	_____ Markers (all necessary colors)
_____ Pencils	_____ Computers	
	_____ Projection	

Meeting Hints: Dos and Don'ts

Do
1. Be sure the meeting is necessary.
2. Be sure all the appropriate people are notified in writing.
3. Be sure the agenda has been prepared and circulated.
4. Be sure each participant knows what she/he is supposed to bring and to do.
5. Start on time and end on time.
6. Keep minutes to summarize what happens.
7. Identify the person in charge.
8. Use an off-site facility if possible.

Don't
1. Put more on the agenda than can be covered.
2. Have the meeting at an inappropriate facility.
3. Fail to check on the availability of needed services.
4. Forget to have appropriate food service.
5. Create unnecessary problems of transportation or parking.
6. Allow any one participant to dominate.
7. Allow any participant to be anonymous.
8. Have spouses at the meeting.

Business Plan Coordination Time Chart

0003.doc

Task	Responsible Person	Due Date*
1. Gather background data, including plans, budgets, financial statements, and performance evaluations for past five years (if available).		
2. Level 1		
3. Level 2		
4. Level 3		
5. Level 4		
6. Level 5		
7. Level 6		
8. Level 7		
9. Level 8		
10. Written presentation		
11. Oral presentation		
12. Level 9		

Level 1

Vision

0101.doc

Who: _____

_____

_____

_____

What: _____

_____

_____

_____

When: _____

_____

_____

_____

Where: _____

_____

_____

_____

How Long: _____

_____

_____

_____

Level 1

Planning Process Assumptions—Vision

0102.doc

Since the planning process deals with creating outcomes by future actions, it is essential and necessary to make assumptions about events and circumstances outside the planners' control. These assumptions are critical to the plan.

Please complete this sheet for each key assumption you make.

Assumption	Probability of Assumption Being Violated	Impact if Assumption Violated

Return a copy of this sheet to the plan facilitator who will provide a copy to the next level planners.

Visioning Questions

1. What are our current core competencies? _____

_____

2. What can we leverage to build our future?_____

_____

3. How will the political environment in which we operate change in the next 10 years, and what impact will this have on our organization? _____

_____

4. How will the business environment in which we operate change in the next 10 years, and what impact will this have on our organization? _____

_____

5. What technological changes will impact our organization? What will these changes do to us? _____

_____

6. How can we capitalize on them? _____

_____

7. Who are the people that will lead the organization over the next 10 years?

_____

8. What are their best skills? _____

_____

9. Where will they want to take the organization?_____

_____

10. How big should the organization be? _____

_____

11. What resources will be necessary to achieve this size? _____

_____

12. What knowledge and skills do we organizationally possess that produce a competitive advantage for us? _____

_____

Philosophy and Mission

0201.doc

Who: _____

_____

_____

_____

What: _____

_____

_____

_____

When: _____

_____

_____

_____

Where: _____

_____

_____

_____

How Long: _____

_____

_____

_____

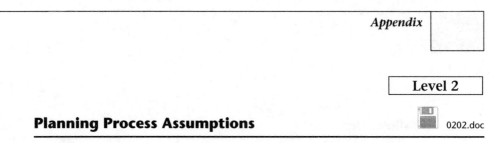

Level 2

Planning Process Assumptions

0202.doc

Since the planning process deals with creating outcomes by future actions, it is essential and necessary to make assumptions about events and circumstances outside the planners' control. These assumptions are critical to the plan.

Please complete this sheet for each key assumption you make.

Assumption	Probability of Assumption Being Violated	Impact if Assumption Violated

Return a copy of this sheet to the plan facilitator who will provide a copy to the next level planners.

Philosophy

0203.doc

Rank

_____ Profits

_____ Customers

_____ Employees

_____ Management

_____ Community

_____ Integrity

_____ Growth

_____ Planning

_____ _____

_____ _____

Level 2

Suggestions for Use

Philosophy

1. The list of topics may not be complete. Add different topics if appropriate.
2. Rank the topics in order of their importance to the company. Compare your ranking with others and discuss the differences.
3. Working with others, attempt to assemble a master list of topics and rankings upon which you can agree.
4. Working with others, write a short statement about each topic. It might follow the form: "We believe that . . . ; therefore, . . ." It usually helps later in the planning process to have included the *therefore,* since it can provide something to act upon.
5. Test the statements produced by asking employees to read them and then describe what changes might be produced in their jobs by acting on them. If few changes are suggested, you have probably done an excellent job of communicating or else the statements are in need of reconsideration.
6. Order the statements by the ranks assigned in suggestion 2, print them, and distribute them to employees before requesting their participation in the planning process.

Level 2

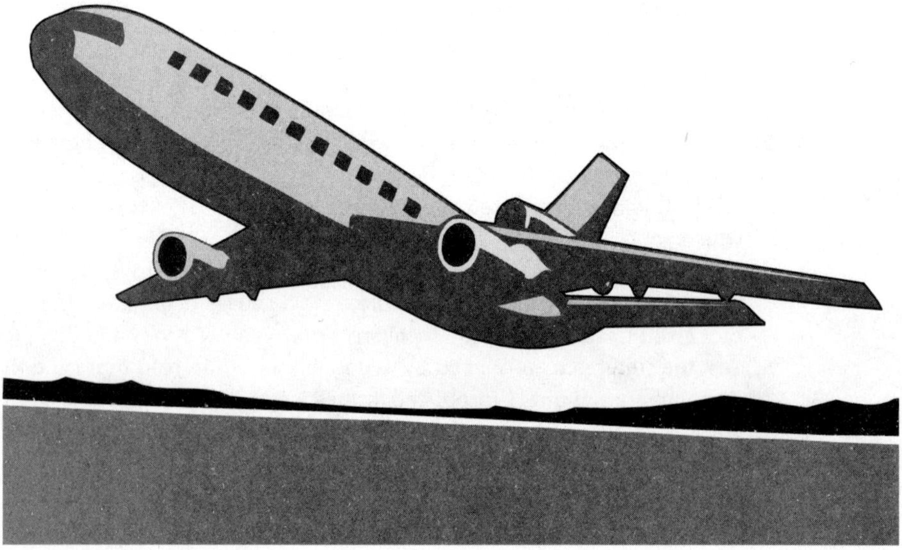

What Do We Do Best?

0204.doc

1904   Window Shades
Today _____

What Need Do We Meet?

0205.doc

_____

_____

_____

_____

_____

_____

_____

_____

Level 2

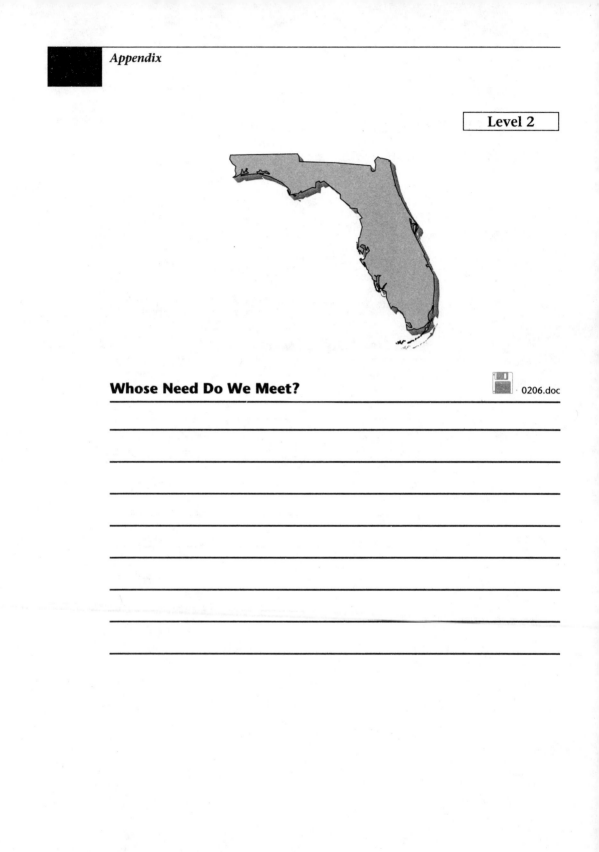

Whose Need Do We Meet?

0206.doc

_____

_____

_____

_____

_____

_____

_____

_____

Suggestions for Use

What Business Are We In?

1. Answer question 1, considering both:
   a. What do we do better than anything else we do?
      and
   b. What do we do better than anyone else who does it?
2. Answer question 2, considering needs at a basic level and not a need for product or service.
3. Answer question 3, considering not just with whom you may come into contact, but also:
   a. Who really derives the benefits or has needs met?
      and
   b. Who actually pays and why are they willing to pay?
4. Answer question 4 by combining the answers to the first three questions. It may be possible to do this in one sentence. This answer may constitute your mission statement.
5. If your company is actually in several businesses, it is best to write a mission statement for each and add a statement describing the so-called glue which holds them together.
6. You may wish to add to the mission statement a description of the path the business may follow while growing. Growth could be along present lines, or it could require considerable change.

What Business Are We In?

0207.doc

1. What do we do best?

_____

_____

_____

_____

_____

2. What need do we meet?

_____

_____

_____

_____

3. Whose need do we meet?

_____

_____

_____

_____

_____

4. What business are we in?

_____

_____

_____

_____

_____

Mission Statements

General Examples

One of the major manufacturers in the United States has published the following:

> *Our mission is to improve continually our products and services to meet our customers' needs, allowing us to prosper as a business and to provide a reasonable return for our stockholders, the owners of our business.*

A wholesale distributor has stated:

> *We are in the business of providing on-time delivery of products which satisfy end user specifications and provide profitable margins to our distributors.*

A company with a bent for engineering among the senior managers determined:

> *We are in the business of profitably designing, manufacturing, marketing, and supporting products in which we have a value-added component.*

A small entrepreneurial operation wrote:

> *We are in the business of producing for elementary grade children supplementary learning materials which meet the following criteria:*
> - *integrate and coordinate with basic texts for skill development*
> - *are adaptable to student progress at the individual level*
> - *have been designed and tested by teachers*

A new business development group of a professional services firm thought:

> *We are in the business of creating new profit centers.*

An international, very large, specialty chemical company says:

> *Our mission is to balance value for our other constituencies with maximizing long-term shareholder value.*

An international manufacturer of components and controls writes:

> *We produce products of high quality and value in the most competitively priced markets.*

Strategic Plan

0301.doc

Who: _____

_____

_____

_____

What: _____

_____

_____

_____

When: _____

_____

_____

_____

Where: _____

_____

_____

_____

How Long: _____

_____

_____

_____

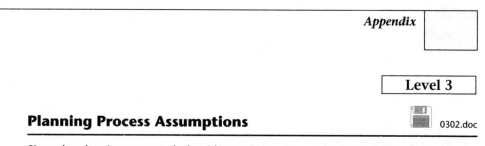

Level 3

Planning Process Assumptions

0302.doc

Since the planning process deals with creating outcomes by future actions, it is essential and necessary to make assumptions about events and circumstances outside the planners' control. These assumptions are critical to the plan.

Please complete this sheet for each key assumption you make.

Assumption	Probability of Assumption Being Violated	Impact if Assumption Violated

Return a copy of this sheet to the plan facilitator who will provide a copy to the next level planners.

SWOT Analysis

1. List the company's strengths. You might consider what you think are the primary internal reasons for the company's past or expected successes.
2. List the company's weaknesses. *This is not negative thinking.* One of the greatest opportunities for future improvement is in correcting these. If this list is not at least as long as the previous list, consider that sometimes a weakness is a strength that is overdone and see if that gives you some ideas.
3. List opportunities. These may or may not also be available to competitors.
4. List threats. Again, these may or may not affect competitors.
5. For each strength, consider:
   a. How can we enhance it?
   b. How can we protect it?
   c. How can we use it to our advantage?
6. For each weakness, consider:
   a. How can we eliminate it?
   b. How can we disguise it?
   c. What does it keep us from doing?
7. For each opportunity, consider:
   a. What prevents us from taking advantage of it?
   b. How could we best take advantage of it?
   c. How long will it likely remain available?
8. For each threat, consider:
   a. What is the worst that is likely to happen?
   b. For how long is the threat likely to continue?
   c. How can we eliminate or minimize its effects?
9. Fill the sheet out again for each major competitor. *This is very important. You are not thinking strategically if you are not thinking about the competition.*

SWOT Analysis

0303.doc

Strengths	Weaknesses

Opportunities	Threats

Level 3

Strategic Factors Analysis

1. Identify specific customer/client or a specific customer/client group. Insert in upper left corner.
2. Identify specific product/service to be offered. Insert in upper right corner.
3. Identify the strategic factors considered important to the identified group in suggestion 1. Enter these as column headings along with *Price, Quality,* and *Delivery.*
4. Rank these strategic factors in order of importance, and enter your numerical results into the column headings labeled *Rank.*
5. Compare answers with others and attempt a consensus.
6. List yourself as the first entry under *Companies;* then, in descending order of market share, continue with a list of your competitors.
7. Compare answers with others and attempt a consensus.
8. Insert numbers into the matrix indicating each competitor's ranking with respect to each strategic factor.
9. Compare answers with others and attempt a consensus.
10. Identify rankings which are likely to be subject to attempts at change or which may be likely to change due to economic environment factors. Identify direction of such changes with arrows.
11. Compare answers with others and attempt a consensus.
12. In the space provided, write a short summary of the above described situation.

Strategic Factors Analysis

0304.doc

Customer/Client   Product/Service

Rank						
Companies	**Price**	**Quality**	**Delivery**			

Summary

Thirty Questions to Assist with Strategic Planning   0305.doc

1. Who are our five major customers (or classes of customers)?
   a. _____
   b. _____
   c. _____
   d. _____
   e. _____

2. What are the common characteristics of these five?
   a. _____
   b. _____
   c. _____

3. Why do they buy our product?
   a. _____
   b. _____
   c. _____

4. Who are three potential customers (or classes of customers) who do not currently do business with us?
   a. _____
   b. _____
   c. _____

5. Why don't these three do business with us?
   a. _____
   b. _____
   c. _____

6. Are there any obvious ethnic, age, religious, gender, or other biases in our customer base?
   _____
   _____

7. What is our most effective sales channel?
   _____
   _____
   _____

8. What products are our three greatest revenue producers?
   a. _____
   b. _____
   c. _____

9. What products are our three greatest profit producers?
   a. _____
   b. _____
   c. _____

10. If customers could not buy what we sell (even from a competitor) what would they do?

_____

_____

_____

_____

_____

Demographics—Who buys?

11. Are our products purchased primarily by any particular age group?

_____

12. Are our products purchased primarily by any specific ethnic group?

_____

13. Are our products purchased primarily by one gender?

_____

14. Are our products purchased primarily within any geographic area(s)?

_____

15. Are our products purchased primarily by any income level group?

_____

16. Are sales of our product(s) tied to sales or use of any other products?

_____

17. Are sales of our product tied largely to any occupational category?

_____

18. What is the education level of our primary purchasers?

_____

19. Who (according to the above categories) are the heaviest users of our products?

_____

Psychographics—Why do they buy?

20. What are the benefits each class of customer (see above) derives from using our product?

_____

_____

21. Which *advertising* has been most effective?

_____

_____

22. Whose *endorsement* might cause a person to buy our product(s)?

_____

_____

23. What types of *packaging* have produced the most sales?

_____

_____

24. What is the buyer's *hot button?*

_____

_____

Channels—Where do they buy?

25. Which distribution channel produces the most sales revenue?

_____

_____

26. Which distribution channel produces the most gross profit?

_____

_____

27. What has been the greatest change competitors have made in distribution channels?

_____

_____

28. What has been the most effective change we have made in distribution channels?

_____

_____

29. Why was the change (in question 28) so effective?

_____

_____

30. Is there a level in the distribution link which can be eliminated?

_____

_____

Level 3

Strategic Plan of Action

0306.doc

With specific reference to your competitors, what do you most want to accomplish? (State the accomplishments as specific results.)

1. _____
   _____

2. _____
   _____
   _____

3. _____
   _____
   _____

What course of action will you follow to cause these to happen?

1. a. _____
      _____
      _____

   b. _____
      _____

   c. _____
      _____
      _____

2. a. _____
      _____

   b. _____
      _____

   c. _____
      _____

3. a. _____
      _____

   b. _____
      _____

   c. _____
      _____
      _____

Level 4

Corporate Objectives

0401.doc

Who: _____

_____

_____

_____

What: _____

_____

_____

_____

When: _____

_____

_____

_____

Where: _____

_____

_____

_____

How Long: _____

_____

_____

_____

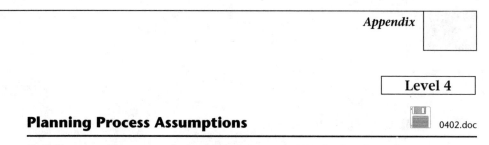

Level 4

Planning Process Assumptions

0402.doc

Since the planning process deals with creating outcomes by future actions, it is essential and necessary to make assumptions about events and circumstances outside the planners' control. These assumptions are critical to the plan.

Please complete this sheet for each key assumption you make.

Assumption	Probability of Assumption Being Violated	Impact if Assumption Violated

Return a copy of this sheet to the plan facilitator who will provide a copy to the next level planners.

History Questionnaire

0403.doc

To be completed by: _____

Completing these questions will help to show how we became what we are and why we are positioned to do what we have planned to do.

1. Date of company's founding. _____

   _____

   _____

2. Original founder(s) of business, name of business, location of business, and purpose of business. _____

   _____

   _____

3. Changes in name, location, and/or purpose, along with corresponding dates.

   _____

   _____

   _____

4. Major economic or environmental events which have affected company.

   _____

   _____

   _____

5. Dates and explanations of major additions to or divestitures of business.

   _____

   _____

   _____

6. Major obstacles and problems the business has faced. _____

   _____

   _____

   _____

7. Turning points and causes of greatest periods of growth and profitability.

   _____

   _____

   _____

Level 4

Evaluation Chart for Planning

1. Solicit suggestions for *Elements*. These should be problems (things that need fixing) that participants in the planning meeting may have control over.
2. Sort elements by *Areas*. Areas can be designated by discretion. The most common areas are products or areas of responsibility. It should be clear who has responsibility for each area.
3. Select four elements for each area and enter them on the chart. Do not use prejudiced words such as *bad* or *late*.
4. Copy the chart and circulate it to those who will attend the meeting. This should be done approximately two weeks before the meeting.
5. Collect the sheets and record on a separate sheet the highest and lowest scores assigned to each element. Copy and distribute this sheet at the meeting.
6. Discuss each element by allowing one minute each to the persons assigning the lowest and highest scores. Next, allow additional comments (limited to one minute) from others who assigned scores—provided they have something to add.
7. Ask the person who assigned the lowest score, "What would you have to see before you could change your score to be five points higher than the highest score?"
8. Record the answer.
9. Move to the next element.

Evaluation Chart for Planning

0404.xls

Areas

100																		
95																		
90																		
85																		
80																		
75																		
70																		
65																		
60																		
55																		
50																		
45																		
40																		
35																		
30																		
25																		
20																		
15																		
10																		
5																		

Instructions: For those elements of which you have knowledge, mark the appropriate square to give a score that answers the question "How are we doing with respect to this element?"

Where Are We?

0405.doc

To be completed by: _____

1. Why are we in business?

   _____

2. What business are we in?

   _____

3. Where are we in the life cycle of the industry?

   _____

4. Where are we in the life cycle of the company?

   _____

5. How did we get here?

   _____

   a. Narrative background of major events

      _____

   b. Historical financial information

      _____

6. What market factors affect us?

   _____

   a. Input side
      • Personnel

      _____

      • Materials

      _____

      • Financing

      _____

      • Equipment

      _____

b. Output side

- Primary customers

  _____

- Secondary customers

  _____

7. What internal factors affect us?

   _____

   a. Our strengths

      _____

   b. Our weaknesses

      _____

8. What other external factors affect us?

   _____

   a. Regulation

      _____

   b. Legislation

      _____

   c. Competition

      _____

Where Are We Going?

0406.doc

To be completed by: _____

1. Who are the *we* referred to above?

_____

2. What alternatives are available to us?

_____

3. Consider the critical issues such as:
   a. Desired rate of growth

   _____

   b. Desired rate of profitability

   _____

   c. Desired public image

   _____

   d. New markets

   _____

   e. New products

   _____

   f. Availability of financing

   _____

   g. Capability of personnel

   _____

   h. Adequacy of plant and equipment

   _____

4. Where will our strengths take us?

_____

5. What are our priorities?

_____

Status Quo Questionnaire

0407.doc

To be completed by: _____

1. If the company operates in the coming year in the same manner as this year, identify those areas under your budgeting control (budget lines) which:
   a. Must be increased

   _____

   b. Could stay the same

   _____

   c. Are targets for cost reductions

   _____

2. Again assuming the present methods of operations:
   a. Identify two conditions over which you have little control that keep your area from making a greater profit contribution.

   _____

   _____

   b. State two changes which you have (or can get) authority to initiate that should make your area more profitable.

   _____

   _____

   c. By what date(s) could the above changes reasonably be made?

   _____

How Do We Get There?

0408.doc

To be completed by: _____

1. What alternative courses are available to us?

   _____

2. What are the pros and cons of each alternative?

   _____

3. Which alternatives match up with our resources and our strengths (path of least resistance)?

   _____

4. What option(s) gives us the greatest future advantage?

   _____

5. Which objective is first priority?

   _____

6. Who will be responsible for each identified course of action?

   _____

7. What time frames should each have?

   _____

8. What is the biggest stumbling block to achieving our objective? Can we break it into more manageable problems?

   _____

9. What major external economic events (devaluations, political overthrows, nationalization, recessions, etc.) do we foresee?

   _____

10. What major internal economic events (acquisitions, divestitures, retirements, product demise, etc.) do we foresee?

    _____

11. What will it cost—dollars, people, dedication, etc.?

    _____

12. Do we have checkpoints and evacuation routes established?

    _____

(continued)

13. Is it consistent with our strategic plan?

    _____

14. Can we monitor and measure our progress?

    _____

15. Does this fit our stated philosophy?

    _____

How Do We Know When We Are There?

0409.doc

To be completed by: _____

1. Do you have a means to quantify your objectives and goals to the maximum extent possible?

   _____

   _____

   _____

   _____

2. Do you have controls built into the planning process?

   _____

   _____

   _____

   _____

3. Can you describe the final product in sufficient detail so that others can clearly picture what you are attempting to accomplish?

   _____

   _____

   _____

   _____

4. Is the performance measure agreed upon?

   _____

   _____

   _____

   _____

Planning the Reports and Controls

Planning the Reports

1. Show the plan
2. Show the actual
3. Show the difference
4. Show period and year to date
5. Determine when to require explanations
6. Explanations include:
   a. Who is responsible?
   b. What caused it?
   c. Should it continue?
   d. What is to be done?
   e. When will it be done?
   f. Should the plan be changed? When?

Planning the Controls

1. What is to happen?
2. When should it happen?
3. When and how will we know if it is going to happen?
4. When and how will we know if it has happened?
5. Can we divide it into a series of events?
6. Are there points where we can reconsider?
7. Who is responsible for making it happen?
8. Who reports?
9. Are reports quantifiable?
10. Are reports verifiable?
11. What are the tolerances?

Level 4

Internal Data Monitoring

 0410.doc

Item Monitored	Last Period	Current Period	Desired Pro Forma
Financial			
1. Profit Margin (Earnings/Sales)			
2. Asset Turnover (Sales/Assets)			
3. Capital Structure (Assets/Equity)			
4. Return on Equity [(1) × (2) × (3)]			
5. Accounts Receivable Turnover (Sales/Accounts Receivable)			
6. Accounts Payable Turnover (Purchases/Accounts Payable)			
7. Current Ratio (Current Assets/Current Liabilities)			
Operational*			
8.			
9.			

*Examples of operational data to be monitored might include:

- Backlog
- Downtime
- Rejects
- Calls received

Sources of External Information

Federal Government
Many of the following and other general statistical sources can be found at
www.lib.utulsa.edu/guides/stage2.htm

1. Statistical Abstract of the United States
   (U.S. Department of Commerce, Bureau of the Census)
   Issued Annually
   Social, Political, and Economic Statistics
2. Survey of Current Business
   (U.S. Department of Commerce, Bureau of Economic Analysis)
   Issued Monthly
   Business Indicators, Domestic & Foreign Trade, Prices, Labor & Employment,
      Raw Materials
3. Economic Indicators
   (Superintendent of Documents, Government Printing Office)
   Issued Monthly
   Government Printing Office
   www.access.gpo.gov
4. Bureau of Census has several publications which are very helpful with demographics
   but most are issued on a ten-year cycle.
   www.census.gov
5. Federal Reserve Bulletin
   (Board of Governors of the Federal Reserve System)
   Issued Monthly
   Board of Governors' page has links to all federal reserve banks.
   www.bog.frb.fed.us

State Governments
State departments of commerce have data with a more local and regional orientation.
They can be especially helpful in gathering information on the availability and price of
labor.
   Generally, substitute the state postal abbreviation in the following example
address which is given for Tennessee (TN).
www.state.tn.us

Computer Accessible Data Bases
1. Data Courier, Inc., Louisville, Kentucky
   ABI/INFORM
2. The Center for Vocational Education, Ohio State University, Columbus, Ohio
   AIM/ARM

3. Arthur D. Little Decision Resources, Cambridge, Massachusetts
   Arthur D. Little/Online
   www.arthurdlittle.com/cybrary/cybrary home.html

4. Business International Corporation, New York, New York
   BI/DATA Forecasts
   BI/DATA Timeseries

5. Bureau of Labor Statistics, United States Department of Labor, Washington, D.C.
   BLS Consumer Price Index
   BLS Employment, Hours, and Earnings
   BLS Labor Force
   BLS Producer Price Index
   //stats.bls.gov

6. Dun's Marketing Services, Parsippany, New Jersey
   D&B Dun's Market Identifiers 10+
   D&B Million Dollar Directory
   D&B Principal International Business
   www.dnb.com

7. Disclosure Incorporated, Bethesda, Maryland
   Disclosure II
   www.disclosure.com

8. Gale Research Company, Detroit, Michigan
   Encyclopedia of Associations
   www.gale.com
   Government data bases may be found at
   www.lsu.edu/guests/manship/classes/mc4971/data dir.html

9. Reports and Studies Index, Find/SVP, New York, New York
   Find/SVP
   www.findsvp.com

10. Bureau of National Affairs, Inc., Washington, D.C.
    Laborlaw
    www.bna.com

11. Predicasts, Inc., Cleveland, Ohio
    PTS Annual Reports Abstracts
    PTS F&S Indexes
    PTS International Forecasts
    PTS International Timeseries
    PTS Prompt
    PTS U.S. Forecasts
    PTS U.S. Timeseries
    Access available through subscribing libraries such as
    www.lib.duke.edu/databases/descriptions/fands.html

12. United States Department of Commerce, Washington, D.C.
    U.S. Exports
    Trade Opportunities
    www.stat-usa.gov

Lists of other resources may be found at:
www.umuc.edu/library/business.html
www.educaid.org/~chadwick/references/interbus.htm

Trade Associations
Besides periodicals and published studies, personal contact can be helpful here. Prepublication information and even that which is not to be published is sometimes available. Many have Internet presences.

Trade Publications
These publications are especially helpful for their (usually) annual statistical issues. May have data available on-line.

Planning Unit Goals

0501.doc

Who: _____

_____

_____

_____

What: _____

_____

_____

_____

When: _____

_____

_____

_____

Where: _____

_____

_____

_____

How Long: _____

_____

_____

_____

Planning Process Assumptions

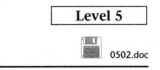 0502.doc

Since the planning process deals with creating outcomes by future actions, it is essential and necessary to make assumptions about events and circumstances outside the planners' control. These assumptions are critical to the plan.

Please complete this sheet for each key assumption you make.

Assumption	Probability of Assumption Being Violated	Impact if Assumption Violated

Return a copy of this sheet to the plan facilitator who will provide a copy to the next level planners.

Input Factors Analysis Instructions

This sheet is to help you determine information you may need to properly develop your planning unit goals. In the left column labeled Item are listed the input factors of production: Personnel, Financing, Materials, and Equipment (sometimes called men, money, materials, and machines). We have listed some generic subfactors under the first two.

Consider the following as an example:

Item	Information	Indicator	Source
Technical Personnel	Availability of people in our area qualified for entry level repair job.	Number of people graduating with AA or BA in Computer Science.	Placement offices of the following schools:

Choose the most significant factors of production to you. Then complete this sheet as in the above example. Assign someone the task of gathering the required information.

Input Factors Analysis

0503.doc

Item	Information	Indicator	Source
Personnel: • Management • Technical • Supervisory • Production • Support			
Financing: • Long-term debt • Long-term equity • Short-term			
Materials:			
Equipment:			

Input Factors Anticipation Instructions

This sheet is most likely to be completed by those with purchasing responsibility. While it is quite detailed, it can be very helpful. You can use it to be sure that all appropriate people are notified not only of changes in raw materials or components used in the manufacturing process, but also of the anticipated effects of those changes.

Level 5

Input Factors Anticipation

0504.doc

Planning Unit _____

To be completed by: _____
Item _____
Annual Quantity _____
Seasonal Variations _____
Acceptable Substitute _____
_____
_____
_____
_____

	Sources	
	Primary:	Secondary:
Price Range		
Lead Time		
Availability		

_____
_____
_____
_____

Anticipated Effects of Using Secondary Source or Substitute:

Costs _____
Quality _____
Sales/Marketing _____
Production _____
Personnel _____
_____
_____
_____
_____

Output Factors Anticipation Instructions

Having looked at the input side of the equation, we now turn to the output side. This sheet is simply a way of accumulating and systematizing your thinking.

You may want to provide copies of this to others in your planning unit and ask them to complete it and return it to you.

Output Factors Anticipation

0505.xls

Planning Unit _____

To be completed by: _____

	Ours	Competitors				
		1	2	3	4	5
Price Range:						
Previous Year 19						
Current Year 19						
Next Year 19						
Annual Quantity:						
Previous Year 19						
Current Year 19						
Next Year 19						

Describe Anticipated Changes in:

Total Market _____

Market Share _____

Number of Competitors _____
Product Substitutes _____

Advertising Levels _____

Customers _____

Level 5

Product Planning Record Instructions

The Product Planning Record will help you to accumulate and see trend information. For the present year and for the previous two years you can complete the *projected* and *actual* rows for each factor. For the next two years you can only do the *Projected* rows at this time (but of course you can compare them to actual later).

Blanks have been left at the bottom for factors you consider particularly important to you. Such things as *Number of Salespeople, New Territories Opened,* and so forth may be placed here.

Review the information and see what trends are developing and what they mean.

	Level 5

Product Planning Record

0506.xls

Planning Unit _____

To be completed by: _____

Product _____ For Year of 19__

			Year		
			Present		
1) Units Sold	—Actual				
2)	—Projected				
3) Unit Sales Price	—Actual				
4)	—Projected				
5) Unit Variable Cost	—Actual				
6)	—Projected				
7) Unit Gross Margin	—Actual				
8)	—Projected				
9) Total Revenue	—Actual				
10)	—Projected				
11) Promotion Expense	—Actual				
12)	—Projected				
13)					
14)					
15)					
16)					

Problems may be indicated by:

- Declining number of units sold
- Declining total revenue
- Declining margins

- Increasing price reductions to maintain sales
- Increasing costs as a percentage of sales

- Increasing promotion expense as a percentage of sales
- Significant variances between actuals and projections

Salesperson's Sales Forecast Instructions

If you have responsibility for sales personnel you may want to use the Salesperson's Sales Forecast sheet. Require each salesperson to complete one sheet for each customer (or class of customer). Note that the form requests the salesperson to commit by quarter how much of each product he/she will sell to the customer.

The sheet should be completed in units, not dollars.

Obviously, this sheet helps to determine manufacturing flow, inventory levels, and cash flow.

Note that this sheet can also be used by service firms. The *Units Projected* will become billable hours and the *Product(s)* can be specific people or specific talents/skills.

Level 5

Salesperson's Sales Forecast for 19___

0507.xls

Planning Unit

To be completed by: _____

Customer   Salesman

Product(s)	Quarter 1	Quarter 2	Quarter 3	Quarter 4	Annual
_____					
_____					
_____					
_____					
_____					
_____					
_____					
_____					
_____					
_____					
_____					
_____					
_____					
_____					
Totals					

Units Projected

- Summarize by division
- Summarize by product

Sales Forecast Summary Instructions

The Sales Forecast Summary is used to consolidate all of the information submitted on the Salesperson's Sales Forecast. After appropriate consideration (and adjustments, if necessary), it should be a good foundation for planning the production.

Sales Forecast Summary for 19__

0508.xls

| | Planning Unit |
To be completed by: _____

Units Projected

Product(s)	Quarter 1	Quarter 2	Quarter 3	Quarter 4	Annual
_____					
_____					
_____					
_____					
_____					
_____					
_____					
_____					
_____					
_____					
_____					
_____					
_____					
_____					
Totals					

Value Analysis Grid Instructions

We have chosen to put *Price* and *Quality* on the axis of the Value Analysis Grid. You may choose other factors if you deem them more important (Service, Components of Quality, etc.). Whatever you choose, keep the value concept foremost.

Choose a specific product or service to analyze. Determine where you think you are on the grid. Then place your strongest competitors on the grid. Also, look at the change in volume of business that each of you is doing.

For anyone (including yourself) not on the *Value Line,* try to determine how they got there, whether they want to be there, and what their next likely move will be.

Value Analysis Grid

0509.xls

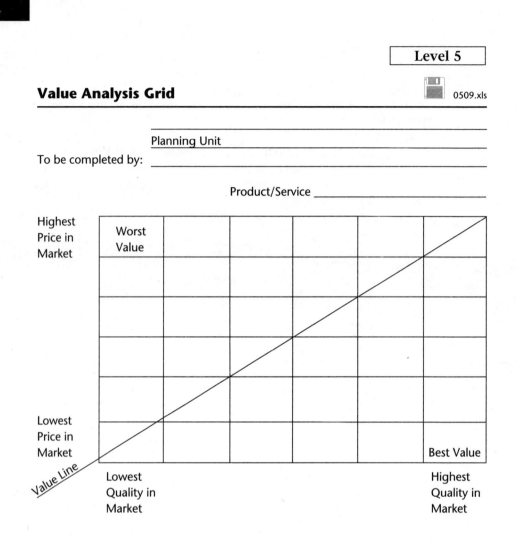

Planning Unit

To be completed by:

Product/Service

	Worst Value				
Highest Price in Market					
Lowest Price in Market					Best Value

Value Line

Lowest Quality in Market   Highest Quality in Market

Planning Unit Goal Sheet

0510.doc

Objective _____   _____

_____

Goal _____   _____

_____

Present Status (/   /   )

_____

_____

_____

_____

Resource Requirements

_____

_____

_____

_____

Responsible Individual _____

Estimated Completion Date _____

Concurring Managers _____   _____

Authorized Approval _____

Comments _____

_____

_____

_____

Level 5

0511.xls

EXHIBIT 5.12

Outline of Planned Changes

#	Goals	Expected Results	$	Resources Required	$	Timelines			
						1st Qtr.	2nd Qtr.	3rd Qtr.	4th Qtr.
1	Increase Productivity	5% decrease in Direct Labor	1 MM	1 Press	500 K				

Tactics and Projections

0601.doc

Who: _____

_____

_____

_____

What: _____

_____

_____

_____

When: _____

_____

_____

_____

Where: _____

_____

_____

_____

How Long: _____

_____

_____

_____

| Level 6 |

Planning Process Assumptions

0602.doc

Since the planning process deals with creating outcomes by future actions, it is essential and necessary to make assumptions about events and circumstances outside the planners' control. These assumptions are critical to the plan.

Please complete this sheet for each key assumption you make.

Assumption	Probability of Assumption Being Violated	Impact if Assumption Violated

Return a copy of this sheet to the plan facilitator who will provide a copy to the next level planners.

Goal Action Plan Sheet Instructions

This sheet is critical to the success of the plan. Up to this point the effort has focused on what is to be accomplished. Now you must show exactly how it will be accomplished.

You should call a meeting of your direct reports, those who will be assigned the responsibility of getting done the tasks that will accomplish your goals. Present them with copies of the Goal Sheet and of the Goal Action Plan Sheet (including the examples).

You must now decide what specific things must be done (*Tactics/Action Steps*), who will get them done (*Responsible Person*), how you will know when they are done (*Projections/Evidence of Completion*), and when they will be done (*Timeline*). For the moment, leave the *Status/Comments* column blank. Put an identification of the goal for which this is the action plan in the lower left corner (by number or brief description).

Decide on this information with your reports and complete one form for each goal.

Goal Action Plan Sheet

0603.xls

#	Tactics/ Action Steps	Responsible Person	Status/ Comments	Projections/ Evidence of Completion	Year
					J F M A M J J A S O N D

Goal _____

	Year
Report Date	J F M A M J J A S O N D
Date	
Initials	

Level 6

Individual Accountability and Action Plans

0604.xls

Name _____

Position _____

Evaluator _____ Date: _____

Approved by _____ Date: _____

Individual Accountability:

Individual Action Items:

Measurements:

Performance Evaluation of Accountability:

(   ) More than   (   ) Satisfactory   (   ) Less than
        Satisfactory   Satisfactory

Individual Performance Evaluation

0605.xls

Name _____

Position _____

Dates of Review Period __/__/__ to __/__/__

Summary of Performance Evaluation:
( ) More than   ( ) Satisfactory   ( ) Less than
    Satisfactory   Satisfactory

Too New to Evaluate:
( ) Satisfactory Progress   ( ) Unsatisfactory Progress

Action Plan Summary: (Use additional sheets if necessary)

Strong Points _____

_____

_____

Weak Points _____

_____

_____

Plan for Development _____

_____

_____

Evaluator's Signature _____ Date _____
Approved by _____ Date _____

Accountabilities Established:
    ( ) Accountabilities have been established for the upcoming period.
Evaluator's Signature _____ Date _____
Approved by _____ Date _____

Budgeting

0701.doc

Who: _____

_____

_____

_____

What: _____

_____

_____

_____

When: _____

_____

_____

_____

Where: _____

_____

_____

_____

How Long: _____

_____

_____

_____

Planning Process Assumptions

0702.doc

Since the planning process deals with creating outcomes by future actions, it is essential and necessary to make assumptions about events and circumstances outside the planners' control. These assumptions are critical to the plan.

Please complete this sheet for each key assumption you make.

Assumption	Probability of Assumption Being Violated	Impact if Assumption Violated

Return a copy of this sheet to the plan facilitator who will provide a copy to the next level planners.

Coordination

0801.doc

Who: _____

_____

_____

_____

What: _____

_____

_____

_____

When: _____

_____

_____

_____

Where: _____

_____

_____

_____

How Long: _____

_____

_____

_____

Level 8

Planning Process Assumptions

0802.doc

Since the planning process deals with creating outcomes by future actions, it is essential and necessary to make assumptions about events and circumstances outside the planners' control. These assumptions are critical to the plan.

Please complete this sheet for each key assumption you make.

Assumption	Probability of Assumption Being Violated	Impact if Assumption Violated

Return a copy of this sheet to the plan facilitator who will provide a copy to the next level planners.

Plan Change Process

0803.doc

This plan will be reviewed quarterly by its preparers. The review meeting will be held in the _____ week after the end of the quarter. The meeting will be called and the location, time, and agenda set by _____.
Included in the agenda will be:

1. A review of results obtained
2. A review of assumptions
3. A review of performance vs. plan
4. Suggested changes

   Those having suggestions for additional agenda items should submit them at least one week before the meeting.
   Changes approved in the meeting will be included in the plan book with changes to appropriate pages.

Date of Change	Pages Changed	Reasons for Change

Level 9

Implementation and Follow-up

0901.doc

Who: _____

_____

_____

_____

What: _____

_____

_____

_____

When: _____

_____

_____

_____

Where: _____

_____

_____

_____

How Long: _____

_____

_____

_____

Planning Process Assumptions

0902.doc

Since the planning process deals with creating outcomes by future actions, it is essential and necessary to make assumptions about events and circumstances outside the planners' control. These assumptions are critical to the plan.

Please complete this sheet for each key assumption you make.

Assumption	Probability of Assumption Being Violated	Impact if Assumption Violated

Return a copy of this sheet to the plan facilitator who will provide a copy to the next level planners.

Individual Performance Expectations—Instructions

Due Date   Planning Facilitator

Each Responsible Manager should complete an Individual Performance Expectations (IPE) sheet for each employee to whom one or more Action Steps has been assigned for one or more Goals.

Primarily, the IPE sheet is a consolidation of information from the Goal Action Plan Sheets. It is intended to help the employee and manager understand and track the Tactics/Action Steps for which an individual is responsible.

As the Responsible Manager, you should:

1. Complete the Name and Department information.
2. List the Goal ID #, the Tactic/Action Step Assigned, the Completion Date by which this step should be done, and the Evidence of Completion for *each* item assigned to this person. This information can be taken from the Goal Action Plan Sheets.
3. Complete the "Page __ of __" indicators for each page for each person.
4. Give a copy of each Employee's IPE to that Employee and discuss the expectations.
5. Have each employee sign and date (Acknowledged by and Date) the original IPE and return it to you. The employee should retain a copy.
6. Keep a copy and give the original to the Planning Coordinator by the Due Date.
7. At least quarterly, review the IPE sheets with each of your employees as a part of the plan progress review.

Level 9

Individual Performance Expectations—Summary of Tactics/ Action Steps Assigned

0903.xls

Name: _____   Page __ of __

Department: _____   Acknowledged by: _____

Date: _____

Goal ID #	Tactic/Action Step Assigned	Completion Date	Evidence of Completion

Corporate Objectives

WEIGHTING SHEET

FYE: _____

INSTRUCTIONS

_____   _____
Due Date   Planning Facilitator

Attached is the Corporate Objectives Weighting Sheet. Columns 1 and 2 have been completed for you.

Please review these Objectives, as previously established by Senior Management, and assign weights (portion of 100%) to each one that reflects your interpretation of the relative importance of that objective. You may feel that all should be evenly weighted. Or, you may wish to assign heavier weights to some than others.

NOTE: The total of all assigned weights must be 100%.

This information will be aggregated and final weights will be assigned to the Objectives.

Corporate Objectives

0904.xls

WEIGHTING SHEET
FYE: _____

Due Date

Planning Facilitator

Col. 1	Col. 2	Col. 3
Number	Statement of the Objective	Weight
XXXXXXXXX	XXXXXXXXXXXXXXXXXXXXXXXXXXXXXXXX	100%

Level 9

Goal Listing Sheet

0905.xls

FYE: _____

Manager: _____

Goal Identification #	Goal Statement

Goal Weighting and Progress Chart

FYE: _____

INSTRUCTIONS

_____   _____
Due Date   Planning Facilitator

You have received a summary of all the Goals for your responsibility area with a Goal Identification number assigned and a Goal Weighting and Progress Chart listing all your Goals by Identification Number. If this is not so, please contact the Planning Facilitator immediately.

The Goal Listing Sheet is a summary of the Goals you have established for yourself and your responsibility area. It is for your information.

Goal Weighting and Progress Chart Instructions:

1. Columns 1, 2, and 3 have been completed for you.
2. Looking at your Goal Listing Sheet and considering the weight assigned to the related Corporate Objectives, (Col. 2), assign a weight (portion of 100%) to each listed Goal. Place the assigned weight in Col. 4 beside each Goal number (Col. 3).
3. Note that the sum of all Goal Weights for your Department must be 100%.
4. For each listed Goal, complete Cols. 5, 7, and 9 with the **cumulative** percentage of that Goal which you plan to attain by the end of the indicated quarter. Note that Col. 11 already indicates the planned cumulative percentage completion at the end of the 4th quarter to be 100%.
5. The same sheet will be used at the end of each quarter for you to record the Actual Completion of each Goal. However, at this time, Cols. 6, 8, 10, and 12 should be left blank.
6. When you have completed the above, make a copy of this sheet for your records and return the original to the Planning Facilitator by the Due Date above.

Level 9

Goal Weighting and Progress Chart

0906.xls

FYE: _____

_____   _____
Due Date   Planning Facilitator

Please complete the indicated columns and return to the Planning Facilitator on or before the Due Date.

Columns to be Completed

Responsible Person: _____ | 1 | 2 | 3 | 4 | 5 | 6 | 7 | 8 | 9 | 10 | 11 | 12 |

Corp. Obj. No.	Weight to Objective	Goal No.	Weight to Goal	Exp. 1st Qtr.	Act. 1st Qtr.	Exp. 2nd Qtr.	Act. 2nd Qtr.	Exp. 3rd Qtr.	Act. 3rd Qtr.	Exp. 4th Qtr.	Act. 4th Qtr.
										100%	
										100%	
										100%	
										100%	
										100%	
										100%	
										100%	
										100%	
										100%	
										100%	
										100%	
										100%	
										100%	
XX	XX	XX	100%	XX	XX	XX	XX	XX	XX	XX	XX
Col 1	Col 2	Col 3	Col 4	Col 5	Col 6	Col 7	Col 8	Col 9	Col 10	Col 11	Col 12

*Exp = Expected at beginning of plan year *Act = Actual at end of quarter
Expected columns to be completed fully. Actual columns to be completed at the end of the quarter.

Goal Weighting and Progress Chart

FYE: _____

First Quarter Instructions

Due Date   Planning Facilitator

Attached is a copy of a Goal Weighting and Progress Chart for you. Columns 1, 2, 3, 4, 5, 7, 9, and 11 are completed.

You are to complete Column 6 which is your evaluation of the Actual Completion Percentage on each of your Goals as of the end of Quarter 1.

Return the Goal Weighting and Progress Chart sheet to the Planning Facilitator by the Due Date.

Goal Weighting and Progress Chart

FYE: _____

Second Quarter Instructions

Due Date   Planning Facilitator

Attached is a copy of a Goal Weighting and Progress Chart for you. Columns 1, 2, 3, 4, 5, 6, 7, 9, and 11 are completed.

You are to complete Column 8 which is your evaluation of the Actual Completion Percentage on each of your Goals as of the end of Quarter 2.

Return the Goal Weighting and Progress Chart sheet to the Planning Facilitator by the Due Date.

Goal Weighting and Progress Chart

FYE: _____

Third Quarter Instructions

Due Date   Planning Facilitator

Attached is a copy of a Goal Weighting and Progress Chart for you. Columns 1, 2, 3, 4, 5, 6, 7, 8, 9, and 11 are completed.

You are to complete Column 10 which is your evaluation of the Actual Completion Percentage on each of your Goals as of the end of Quarter 3.

Return the Goal Weighting and Progress Chart sheet to the Planning Facilitator by the Due Date.

Goal Weighting and Progress Chart

FYE: _____

Fourth Quarter Instructions

Due Date   Planning Facilitator

Attached is a copy of a Goal Weighting and Progress Chart for you. Columns 1, 2, 3, 4, 5, 6, 7, 8, 9, 10, and 11 are completed.

You are to complete Column 12 which is your evaluation of the Actual Completion Percentage on each of your Goals as of the year-end.

Return the Goal Weighting and Progress Chart sheet to the Planning Facilitator by the Due Date.

Level 9

Comparison of Expected to Actual—Sample

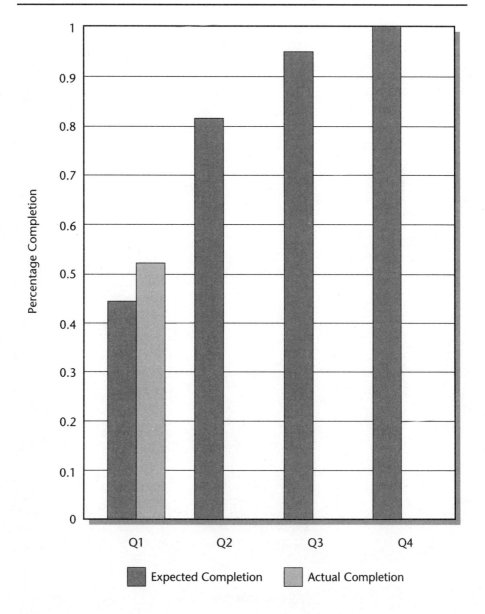

Comparison of Expected to Actual—Sample

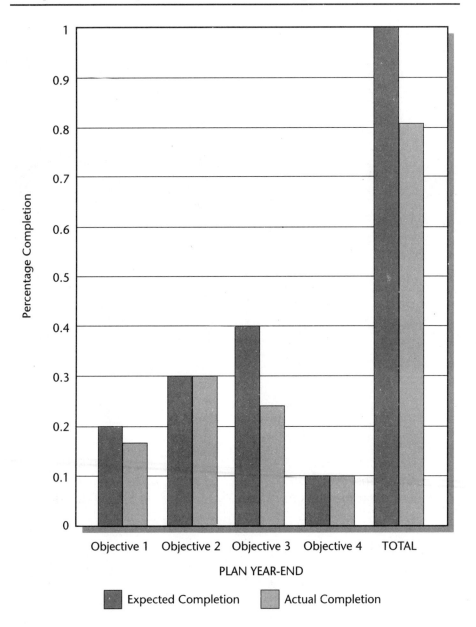

About the Disk

Disk Table of Contents

Title	File Name	Book p. #
Level 9		
Individual Performance Expectations	0903.xls	121,227
Corporate Objectives Weighting Sheet	0904.xls	123,229
Goal Listing Sheet	0905.xls	125,230
Goal Weighting and Progress Chart	0906.xls	126,232

Introduction

The forms on the enclosed disk are saved in Microsoft Word for Windows version 97 and Microsoft Excel version 97. In order to use the forms, you will need to have word processing software capable of reading Microsoft Word for Windows version 97 files, and spreadsheet software capable of reading Microsoft Excel version 97 files.

PowerPoint files may be found on the following web site. http://www.wiley.com/products/subject/accounting/accounting/public/ burton.html

System Requirements

- IBM PC or compatible computer
- 3.5" floppy disk drive
- Windows 95 or later
- Netscape® Navigator 2.0 or later or Microsoft Internet Explorer 3.0 or later (needed to view PowerPoint files).
- Microsoft Word for Windows version 97 or later or other word processing software capable of reading Microsoft Word for Windows 97 files.

  NOTE: Many popular word processing programs are capable of reading Microsoft Word for Windows 97 files. However, users should be aware that a slight amount of formatting might be lost when using a program other than Microsoft Word. If your word processor cannot read Microsoft Word for Windows 97 files, unformatted text files have been provided in the TXT directory on the floppy disk.

- Microsoft Excel version 97 or later or other spreadsheet software capable of reading Microsoft Excel 97 files.

  NOTE: Files are formatted in Microsoft Excel version 97. To use the worksheets with other spreadsheet programs, refer to the user manual that accompanies your software package for instructions on reading Microsoft Excel files.

How to Install the Files onto Your Computer

To install the files follow these instructions:

1. Insert the enclosed disk into the floppy disk drive of your computer.
2. From the Start Menu, choose **Run**.
3. Type **A:\SETUP** and press **OK**.
4. The opening screen of the installation program will appear. Press **OK** to continue.
5. The default destination directory is C:\BURTON. If you wish to change the default destination, you may do so now.
6. Press **OK** to continue. The installation program will copy all files to your hard drive in the C:\BURTON or user-designated directory.

Using the Files

Loading Files

To use the files, launch the appropriate program (word or excel). Select **File, Open** from the pull-down menu. Select the appropriate drive and directory. If you installed the files to the default directory, the files will be located in the C:\BURTON directory. A list of files should appear. If you do not see a list of files in the directory, you need to select **Word Document (*.doc)** or **Microsoft Excel Files (*.xls)** under **Files of Type**. Double click on the file you want to open. Edit the file according to your needs.

Printing Files

If you want to print the files, select **File, Print** from the pull-down menu.

Saving Files

When you have finished editing a file, you should save it under a new file name by selecting **File, Save As** from the pull-down menu.

User Assistance

If you need assistance with installation or if you have a damaged disk, please contact Wiley Technical Support at:

Phone: (212) 850-6753
Fax: (212) 850-6800 (Attention: Wiley Technical Support)
Email: techhelp@wiley.com

To place additional orders or to request information about other Wiley products, please call (800) 225–5945.